SMALL SPACE WORKSHOPS

How to Create & Use a Downsized Workshop
≫**BONUS**: 12 Complete Benchtop Projects

Larry Okrend

COOL
SPRINGS
PRESS

Inspiring | Educating | Creating | Entertaining

Brimming with creative inspiration, how-to projects, and useful information to enrich your everyday life, Quarto Knows is a favorite destination for those pursuing their interests and passions. Visit our site and dig deeper with our books into your area of interest: Quarto Creates, Quarto Cooks, Quarto Homes, Quarto Lives, Quarto Drives, Quarto Explores, Quarto Gifts, or Quarto Kids.

© 2017 Quarto Publishing Group USA Inc.
Photography © 2017 Larry Okrend, unless otherwise specified

First published in 2017 by Cool Springs Press, an imprint of The Quarto Group, 401 Second Avenue North, Suite 310, Minneapolis, MN 55401 USA. T (612) 344-8100 F (612) 344-8692 www.QuartoKnows.com

Cool Springs Press titles are also available at discount for retail, wholesale, promotional, and bulk purchase. For details, contact the Special Sales Manager by email at specialsales@quarto.com or by mail at The Quarto Group, Attn: Special Sales Manager, 401 Second Avenue North, Suite 310, Minneapolis, MN 55401 USA.

10 9 8 7 6 5 4 3 2 1

ISBN: 978-1-59186-689-3

Library of Congress Cataloging-in-Publication Data

Names: Okrend, Larry, author. | Black & Decker Corporation (Towson, Md.), sponsoring body. | Cool Springs Press, author.
Title: Black & Decker small space workshops / Larry Okrend.
Description: Minneapolis, MN, USA : Cool Springs Press, an imprint of The Quarto Group, 2017. | "How to Create & Use a Downsized Workshop. Bonus: 12 Complete Benchtop Projects"--Cover. | Includes index.
Identifiers: LCCN 2017019393 | ISBN 9781591866893 (paperback)
Subjects: LCSH: Workshops. | Workshops--Equipment and supplies.
Classification: LCC TT152 .O37 2017 | DDC 684/.08--dc23
LC record available at https://lccn.loc.gov/2017019393

Acquiring Editor: Mark Johanson
Project Manager: Alyssa Bluhm
Editor: Bryan Trandem
Art Director: Brad Springer
Layout: Danielle Smith-Boldt
Photography: Larry Okrend

Printed in China

NOTICE TO READERS

For safety, use caution, care, and good judgment when following the procedures described in this book. The publisher and BLACK+DECKER cannot assume responsibility for any damage to property or injury to persons as a result of misuse of the information provided.

The techniques shown in this book are general techniques for various applications. In some instances, additional techniques not shown in this book may be required. Always follow manufacturers' instructions included with products, since deviating from the directions may void warranties. The projects in this book vary widely as to skill levels required: some may not be appropriate for all do-it-yourselfers, and some may require professional help.

Consult your local building department for information on building permits, codes, and other laws as they apply to your project.

Contents

Small Space **Workshops**

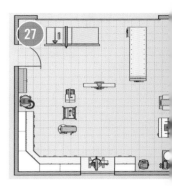

Home shops are often confined to a small corner of a basement, garage, or spare room. The trick to making it work is to have appropriately sized tools and fixtures. A perfectly functional workshop for basic home maintenance and casual woodworking need not take a lot of space.

Finding Inspiration

There are few activities in our busy world that are as useful, affordable, and gratifying as engaging in a traditional craft. They're a stimulating escape from the electronic overload of everyday life—and making objects with our hands unleashes our creativity while serving functional needs. Crafts such as woodworking, carpentry, and metalworking have deep roots and traditions, but also require skills, space, and equipment.

Although all three elements are needed, there's no need to be limited by them. Imagination can overcome many obstacles, and learning how to cope with meager resources can be a liberating experience. Unlike skills that will improve over time, shop space is often finite, so it's necessary to learn to live with what we have. But you can take heart that even those who have expansive shops often find themselves wishing for more space.

This small basement metalworking shop fits entirely against one wall and includes a drafting station for on-the-spot designing. Essential to any workshop, especially one with large power tools, are good lighting and ample electrical service.

Using wall space efficiently is key to making any shop work, and it's particularly important in small spaces where it's essential to minimize intrusions into working space. Here, well-organized hardware bins keep everything in its place, and a set of upper cabinets has been hung slightly lower than normal for easy access and to provide space above for hanging tools. Virtually no wall space is unused here.

The often-quoted rule about the value of real estate, "location, location, location," can be expressed in a slightly different way to understand what it takes to make a small shop successful—"efficiency, efficiency, efficiency." Small shops need:

- Efficient storage
- Efficient layout
- Efficient equipment

Starting with the last item, the scale and number of tools you use must be in sync with the size of your shop. Tools that are too large and too plentiful turn your space into a warehouse rather than a workshop. Of course, an efficient layout depends on efficient equipment, because you need space that allows you to move around (or even swivel on a stool) and produce your projects. And that space needs to support a smooth, logical workflow—materials in, projects out. Every item in your shop needs its own place so you can find it easily and so it doesn't get in the way of work in progress. If you look carefully, you'll find potential storage locations on walls, under benches, and even on the ceiling. There is no shortage of clever commercially available storage systems, or you can devise your own.

Setting up an area along a garage wall may be the most common type of home shop. It needs to be narrow enough to allow cars to park without being damaged. This workbench was custom made for the narrow profile required by the space, with shelves spaced to allow for efficient storage. The space serves mostly general home repair needs and car maintenance.

Shops often need to be flexible for more than one use, and sometimes for several different users. This workshop has an impressive array of hand tools organized in almost obsessive fashion, providing a tool for almost every purpose and every preference. Pegboard is an inexpensive storage solution that can be quickly modified and organized for different crafts.

Repurposing old file cabinets as shop storage is an economical way to keep shop supplies clean and organized. This is a woodworker's shop, where a tall file cabinet with deep drawers is used to store hardware and wood accessories. Ordinary household cabinets and other accessories can be put to good use in a small workshop.

This tuck-under garage shop has a caster-mounted tablesaw for mobility. When the shop isn't being used, the saw can be wheeled against a wall so a lawn tractor can be parked. Extensive storage on the walls and ceiling allow this space to serve many purposes.

It's easy to collect more tools and other items than there's space to store them. This shop could use some organizing; however, part of the appeal of a small shop is to accomplish big things in a small space. Note the dining room buffet cabinet reused as a workbench with storage drawers.

Whether you're a novice DIYer, a crafter, a seasoned woodworker, or a homeowner who's downsizing and in need of a functional workspace, there's a small shop solution that's ideal for your space, budget, and skills. For first-time shop builders, knowing what you need can be a challenge until you have a frame of reference. Perhaps the best way to figure this out is to see what others have done.

An unused closet may be too small for a shop, but it can be an excellent place to store shop supplies to reduce clutter in a working shop space.

This dedicated wood-turning shop is almost entirely contained in a small corner of a basement. All the tools are on mobile bases so they can be easily moved into a working position.

Trying to reinvent the wheel makes no sense when there are so may available solutions for your shop requirements. Many basic design principles are applicable in any shop, so those with small shops can learn from those with large shops and vice versa. Where you locate tools, worksurfaces, and storage depends to a great extent on the type and scale of your projects, but seeing what others have done can be an effective idea incubator. If you already have an established shop, this gallery can provide the inspiration and ideas to change or improve your existing setup—or maybe confirm that you already have it right.

A folding wall cabinet can provide far more storage than a pegboard panel using the same wall space. It's also easy to customize the interior for specific tools. This space belongs to a skilled woodworker with a need for many fine cutting tools.

This basement model-maker's shop occupies a very small corner and manages to use almost every bit of available space. Note the light fixtures mounted on pulleys so the intensity of the light can be adjusted. Such a method could be used in any type of workshop.

Even spacious basement shops like this have many takeaways that apply to small shops, including dust management, mobility, lighting, and wall-storage solutions.

The best spot in your home for a workshop is generally obvious, but in some cases you may need to look a little harder or get extra creative to find a location that meets your needs.

Selecting & Designing Your Space

Choosing and designing a shop space may seem like an intimidating job, but in many respects the process is self-defining once you identify your needs. In most homes, there are only a few appropriate spaces where a workshop can be located, such as a garage or an unfinished basement. The size of the area will probably limit the scope of your projects, so you may need to temper your ambitions with pragmatism.

Once you've settled on the type of work you'd like to accomplish, setting a budget is the next most important step. Your choice of tools, storage units, lighting, and ventilation/heating methods will largely depend on how much you have to spend. If money is no object, for example, there are some excellent shop-specific cabinets and worksurfaces sold at most home centers. A roll-around tool chest is always a good investment, but home-built storage and workbenches offer the best bang for the buck.

It's not uncommon for interests to change or expand as you become a more experienced DIYer, but you need to start somewhere. For example, if you're just starting out in woodworking, simple projects made of plywood, construction lumber, and interior trim boards will help build your skills without breaking the bank. Building storage and fixtures for your new shop is a logical starting point and will help you focus on the types of work you enjoy and can pull off in your new workspace.

Consider using recycled materials and old cabinets. They may not be as appealing as fresh new lumber and shiny new store-bought fixtures, but remember that things quickly get used and dirty in a shop, and anyhow there's nothing wrong with a little "patina" to provide a credible lived-in look. Investing in good tools should be a higher priority than fancy fixtures.

One of the pleasant advantages of a garage or shed shop is the ability to throw open (or roll up) the door in nice weather. Dust and fumes can be blown out with a fan (explosion-proof, if required) and natural light let in for a healthier, more enjoyable work environment.

Planning Considerations

As you get started planning your workshop, let's look at some of the important considerations.

Matching Form to Function

A shop that will be used for simple home repair and maintenance might get by with a large closet or small corner of the garage, while one intended for serious woodworking will need a lot more—in terms of both space and amenities. Your choice of where you put your shop, how much space you devote to it, and what tools and features you put in it will all follow what you plan to use the space for.

How big can a shop be and still be considered small? Although there's no official small-shop size limit, for the purposes of this book a single garage bay (typically about 15 by 20 feet) seems like a reasonable upper limit because many newer homes have an unused or underused third bay. Although the most obvious locations for a shop are in a garage or a basement, you don't need to limit yourself to those spots. Sheds and other outbuildings are particularly functional because they'll contain any mess you might make and keep it out of the house. Although building a shed is an option, you can also buy manufactured sheds in various sizes that are affordable and simple to assemble.

Small-scale projects don't require a large shop, so if that's your focus, even a large closet or a small spare room can be pressed into service. A foldout worksurface and wall-hung cubbies for storage are highly functional for a crafts-oriented shop.

Even if you lack adequate indoor space, a driveway or patio can work as a fair-weather shop for carpentry and woodworking projects. A rolling cart with a worksurface and tool storage is a self-contained shop that also makes a great project.

Considering Others

Out of consideration for the rest of your family, isolation from other living spaces in your home is one of the most important factors in planning a shop, whether you use an existing spot or need to erect walls to create a room. Neighbors in nearby houses should also be considered with shops where noise will be an issue.

Most incorporated communities have ordinances that regulate noise, pollution, zoning, and other factors that may affect how you set up your shop, or even whether you can have one. Of course, you don't want to give the impression that you're operating a commercial shop out of your home so you don't run afoul of the zoning authorities. There may also be neighborhood covenants and restrictions that govern what you can and cannot do on your property. Permits are often required to build new spaces and perform electrical upgrades, and they may require inspections during the process and of the finished work. These are meant to protect you and your neighbors from shoddy and dangerous work, so you should not try to bypass them. Before you sink a lot of time, effort, and money into a shop, you should

Space is at a premium in any small workshop. In this older garage, the owner has built in storage between studs on the unfinished walls.

Although there's no definition of how large a small shop can be, it really depends on how much space you can devote to it. A 15 × 20' single garage bay or a large section of an unfinished basement would typically be the upper end of a residential small shop. You could easily build furniture and cabinets in a shop that size.

research what's allowed in your community. You'll find the information you need online or by calling your local code authority.

Just as important as adhering to code is being considerate of your neighbors by practicing good "shop etiquette." It would be bad form to blow dust and fumes toward your neighbor's kitchen window, or operate noisy machinery at odd hours. If your shop is situated in a place that could disturb your neighbors, it's not a bad idea to let them know when you'll be working and ask whether they might have any concerns. Helping neighbors with their DIY projects and even sharing some of your shop projects with them will go a long way toward the perception that you and your shop are a community asset rather than a nuisance.

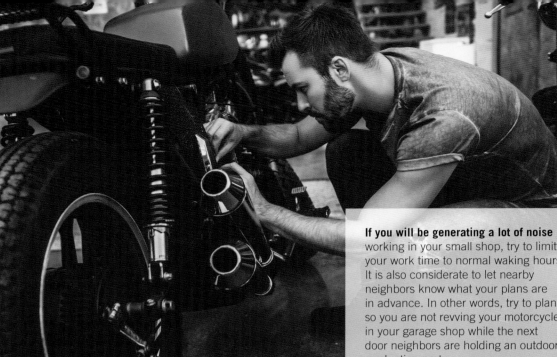

If you will be generating a lot of noise working in your small shop, try to limit your work time to normal waking hours. It is also considerate to let nearby neighbors know what your plans are in advance. In other words, try to plan so you are not revving your motorcycle in your garage shop while the next door neighbors are holding an outdoor graduation party.

Electrical Service

The availability of electrical service is a must—unless you plan on a human-powered, sunlit shop. (Actually, a skylight is a great addition to any shop.) There's typically no need for anything too complex, though. You can easily get by with 20-amp, 110-volt service— the same as what's in most kitchens—if you stick with portable and bench-top power tools. Most bench-top power tools require this level of service. Note that if your current circuit breakers and outlets are 15-amp rated, you should not replace them with 20-amp breakers and outlets, unless you can verify that the current wiring is 12 gauge. Smaller wiring, such as 14 gauge (a larger number equals a smaller gauge), can overheat and potentially be a fire hazard. Large stationary tools, such as a cabinet-shop tablesaw, will likely require upgraded service—a 220-volt circuit and possibly a dedicated breaker box.

For a small shop, it's best to steer clear of large commercial-grade tools. You may be able to get by with one lighting circuit and one wall-outlet circuit. If only one wall outlet is available, you can use a multi-outlet or power strip with a built-in breaker if you don't overtax the circuit. For example, you wouldn't want to run a benchtop tool, an air compressor, and a fan on the same circuit simultaneously. Adding new wiring and circuits becomes necessary if there are no nearby outlets in your chosen shop space, if you plan to run several tools at once, or if you need additional lighting.

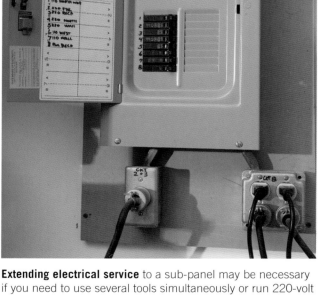

Extending electrical service to a sub-panel may be necessary if you need to use several tools simultaneously or run 220-volt machines. The ability to add a sub-panel depends on the type of service your main electrical panel supports and how many breaker stations are available. This is not a job that most DIYers should attempt to undertake; it should be left to a licensed electrician.

Lighting

Good lighting is essential for working safely. You'll need general lighting and possibly task lighting. Most shops use **overhead fluorescent fixtures** to provide bright, even illumination for most work. But if you want long-lasting flicker-free lights, consider **LED shop lights**. They're initially more expensive than fluorescent tubes but they'll probably never need to be replaced and they can provide a more accurate and pleasing color balance. **Task lights** are helpful when working on small parts or crafts, such as wood turning. The directional light casts shadows, so you can more easily see contours and fine details.

Even if it's too cold to open the door, a skylight can let in natural light year-round. Installing a skylight is a fairly simple DIY job, even one like this with a framed and drywalled shaft. Some skylights can be opened with a crank to provide extra ventilation.

Basements and garages often have fluorescent lighting, and these can be converted to LED lights by removing the ballasts in the light fixtures.

HVAC Needs

A wood shop, which is the most common type of home shop, is often the source of dust and fumes, which can pose health and fire risks that must be addressed. Ideally, the space should be close to an exterior wall for convenient ventilation. However, you can get around this problem to an extent if you use low-VOC water-based finishes and a self-contained dust collection system, such as some shop vacuums. (Remember to always read the directions for finishes to ensure that they're safe to use in your work environment.) Noise reduction is also something to consider if you plan to do a lot of sawing, sanding, and routing. The proximity of your shop to your living space or that of your neighbors will be a determining factor for how much abatement you'll need to do.

Woodworking tends to be an activity that's most often done in the fall and winter months. If you live in an area with "real" winters and work in your garage, you should strongly consider installing a heater. Gas and electric units are the most practical, but a kerosene space heater can work in a pinch. Ideally, the garage walls should be insulated and have drywall to retain the heat. Keep in mind that a heater can ignite dust and fumes, which makes proper ventilation and dust collection even more essential. But in warm weather, a garage has the advantage of being able to leave the overhead door open to reduce the dust and fume problem.

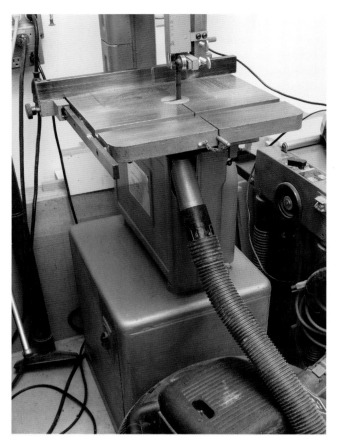

Dust collection is essential for health and safety in a wood shop. A shop vacuum or dust extractor will collect most of the dust produced by portable and bench-top power tools. Larger stationary tools may require a dust collector, which moves a high volume of air and debris.

Shop ventilation not only keeps you more comfortable, but also helps prevent rust from forming on machinery. A wall-mounted oscillating fan may be all you need to keep air moving.

Worksurfaces

Worksurfaces need to be durable but not so hard or rough that they'll damage your work. A traditional maple or birch **butcher-block-style top** is ideal because it can be made smooth and flat, and it's easy to renew if it gets damaged or dirty. You'll find wood tops in various sizes at home centers, at lumberyards, and from online sources. However, it's not the only option.

For less money, you can opt for a **particleboard, plywood**, or **hardboard top**, and these are good choices if you need a sacrificial surface for doing rough work. The best way to make this kind of top is to "sandwich" two or more layers together with screws and then fasten a thin sacrificial hardboard layer on top with a few brads. Fastening layers together will make a flatter, more rigid top. If you do any light-duty metalworking or some forms of craft, such as jewelry making, a metal-clad, stone, or smooth concrete worksurface can be useful.

For fine woodworking projects, a cabinetmaker's bench with a laminated hardwood top affords a solid and precise worksurface. This type of bench should be accessible from all four sides, so it's not a practical choice for a smaller shop.

Most small shops are best served by a shop-built workbench. This is an easy DIY project using construction lumber for the base and plywood or particleboard for the top. The bench's size, features, and location can be customized for your shop.

A small wall-mounted folding workbench can be useful in any shop but especially so in a shared garage where space is at a premium. It's a relatively straightforward project to build out of a single sheet of ¾" × 4 × 8' cabinet-grade plywood. A bench like this is best used for smaller projects and fine work.

Storage Needs

There are many types of suitable shop storage solutions, and each has its advantages and disadvantages. What you choose will depend on budget, preference, and available space. **Pegboard** and **slot wall** (also called slot board and slatwall) are favorites for hanging regularly used tools and other items that you want to be kept readily at hand and organized by task. Although hooks are the most common way to hang tools, there are also brackets available to support shelves and bins. It's a common practice for DIYers to paint a silhouette of the tool in its hanging position so there's never any doubt where it resides. Pegboard is inexpensive, is commonly available, and comes with a good selection of hangers and fixtures. Slot wall has the advantages of having more structural strength and a wider variety of hanging fixtures that can be secured in position, plus it's more attractive than pegboard, but also more expensive.

Floor standing shelves are strong and relatively inexpensive. Metal shelving will support a heavier load, but plastic shelving is lightweight and easy to assemble. Standing shelves offer excellent versatility for storing oddly shaped objects and provide fairly easy access. The downside of both is that they take up floor space that you might otherwise use as a work area or for bench space.

Wall units are one of the most efficient ways to store items such as hardware and portable power tools. DIY shelving is inexpensive and easy to make, but there are size and weight limitations. As a rule of thumb, shelves and cubbies should not be deeper than 12".

A mechanic's tool chest is just as useful for woodworking as it is for auto repair work. It's an ideal place to store tools that are difficult to hang or that need extra protection, and it's helpful for organizing tooling, such as router bits.

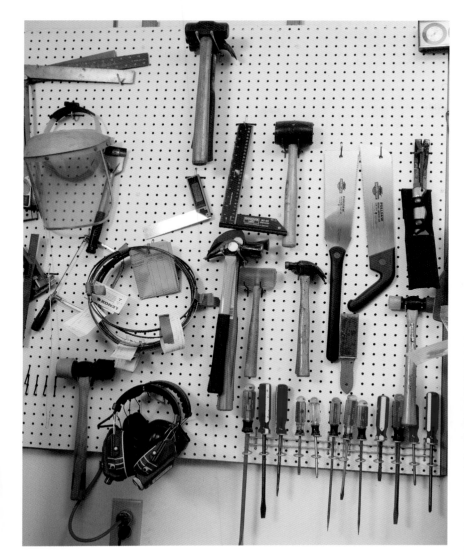

Pegboard may be the most common, least expensive, and most versatile shop storage solution. There are many styles of hooks, bins, and shelves available, and it's easily mounted to walls with cleats. Labels or silhouettes ensure that tools are always returned to the same place.

If your wall space is limited, a cabinet with pegboard doors (left) for tool storage can triple the usable storage area. Because the depth of this cabinet is shallow, it won't intrude into your workspace. A clamp rack (above) that uses depth rather than width for storage can also save wall space.

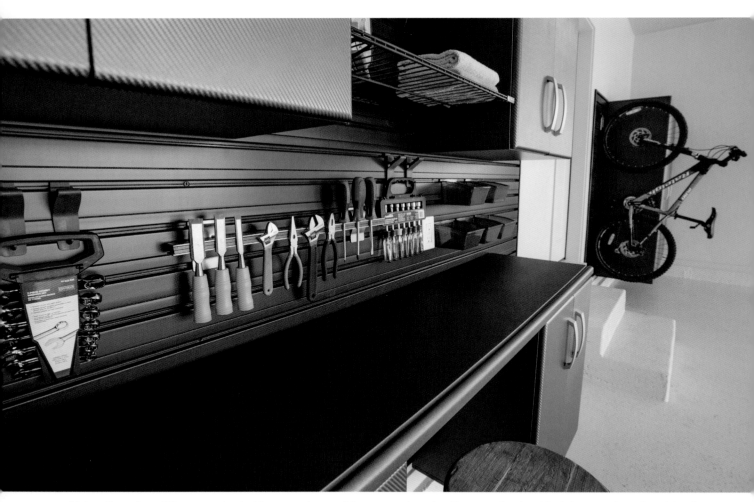

Slat wall can be a little expensive but is a premium wall hanger system, lending a professional look to your shop. A variety of accessories are available to use with such systems. *Image courtesy of Flow Wall®*

Wall shelving may be the least expensive storage solution because you only need brackets, boards, and fasteners. It's typically installed over worksurfaces, and although it's out of the way, it's also harder to reach, so you may need a shop step stool or ladder. This is still a good storage solution for occasionally used items. Of course, any open storage will collect dust, which can become a housekeeping headache.

Cubbies are in the same vein as shelving but they tend to keep things more organized and less cluttered. They're a great way to store hardware items and portable power tools. You can build them yourself out of plywood or use one of the many commercially available systems. You don't need to limit yourself to shop-specific systems; there are organizers designed for closets and kitchens that are just as useful in the shop.

Built-in cabinets with doors and drawers will give your shop a professional vibe—even if they happen to be recycled old kitchen cabinets. They'll provide the most organized, dust-free storage with an uncluttered look, and you can customize the interior to fine-tune their efficiency. However, in a small shop, built-ins can lock you into a particular work style, so you'll want to carefully think through their placement before you install them. If you use volatile finishes and solvents, a fireproof metal storage cabinet is a must-have item and a legal requirement in some communities.

Portable and **rolling storage units** are perhaps the most small-shop-friendly and versatile fixtures, and they also allow the greatest opportunity to customize your shop. A roll-around work cart can have a worksurface that accommodates a variety of bench-top tools and provides storage in its base with drawers, shelves, and bins. Miter saw stands are a small-shop staple, and folding versions are ideal for working at remote job sites. A wall-mounted workbench may not be portable, but because it virtually disappears when stowed, it's a way to keep a multiuse space open. This is an inexpensive and easy-to-build project with plywood and hinges.

High-mounted wall shelving for infrequently used items is inexpensive and easy to build with metal shelf brackets and standard shelving. It's important to note that the brackets should be securely screwed to the wall studs.

Commercially available parts bins are an excellent way to store hardware and shop supplies. Units with transparent boxes allow you to easily categorize and identify items. Wall-mounted units such as this keep clutter off of benches and countertops.

If your shop space is large enough, a dedicated storage area for new and scrap material will keep them out of the way of your workflow. It doesn't need to be fancy; recycled plywood and 2 × 4s work well for building horizontal and vertical stalls.

Comfort & Safety

Working in a shop often requires long hours of standing, which can be hard on your legs and back. Concrete can be particularly fatiguing, and you may feel the need for a more compliant surface. There are a number of ways to add comfort, such as foam and rubber mats, wood overlays (plywood, snap-together flooring, tongue-and-groove flooring), and roll flooring (linoleum, vinyl). Regardless of what you choose, you'll want the surface to be easy to clean and provide good traction. If you're happy standing on concrete (or if you're using mats), coating it with an epoxy garage-floor finish will protect it and make it more attractive while still providing traction. Most hardware stores and home centers sell water-based DIY-friendly epoxy coatings.

If you're building a shop in an unfinished garage, basement, or shed, adding insulation and drywall will help reduce noise, provide more wall-hung storage options, and be brighter and more attractive than bare concrete or open stud bays. It's an inexpensive fix that makes a shop much more livable.

Don't neglect your basic comfort and safety when building your shop. Keep some wall space open for one or more wall-mounted fans and, if possible, an exhaust fan to the outside. They'll help increase air circulation and keep you cooler on hot days. Electrical cords can be a trip hazard, so if it's necessary to route them across the floor, keep them against a wall or use wire raceway. For obvious reasons, you don't want unsupervised kids to have access to your shop, so install locks on doors or on cabinets where you store power tools, cutting tools, and finishes. If something bad does happen, you'll want to be prepared. A first-aid kit and an ABC-rated fire extinguisher are shop essentials.

Your shop's floor plays a big role in comfort, cleanliness, and aesthetics. Clockwise from top left: a wood floor, such as the convenient subfloor panels shown above, is much easier to stand on for long stretches than concrete. Floor mats or roll-out rubber sheeting are good ways to provide additional comfort over any surface. Epoxy coatings provide a surface that's easier to clean than bare concrete and add visual appeal to any shop. Interlocking floor tiles are easy to install and offer some resilience under the feet, relieving fatigue during long working sessions.

Refining Your Plans

Once you've identified a potential shop space, you'll need to check whether it's large enough to accommodate you and the fixtures, storage, worksurfaces, etc.—by creating a layout on graph paper or a grid. The shop will exist in three dimensions, so don't forget about ceiling height. Anything less than an 8-foot ceiling can literally cramp your style. The most efficient layout for most small spaces is to place fixtures on one or two walls and leave the remaining floor space for tasks such as assembling larger projects. In a garage, using an existing wall to attach fold-up worksurfaces and to store rolling fixtures is efficient and should still allow you to park vehicles.

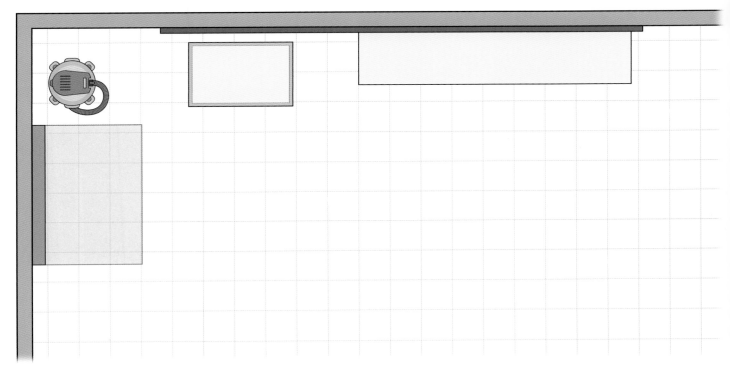

If your shop shares space with your vehicles, it's essential to keep the fixtures and storage as low profile as possible. A fold-down bench protrudes only a few inches when stowed, so it won't encroach on a car's parking spot. The garage's back wall will generally work to house deeper fixtures, such as a rolling cart and a countertop with storage underneath. Pegboard tool storage should work on any wall.

Efficient workflow should be a primary goal of your plan. A small shop may need to use the same worksurface for multiple purposes, such as cutting, assembly, and finishing. Where you store tools and how you use them on a bench (in the case of bench-top tools) should require you to take as few steps and motions as possible. Obviously, the most used items should be the most accessible, and rarely used items can be located in harder to reach places, such as on overhead shelving or cubbies. Being efficient requires keeping the space clean, especially if you do finishing in the same area as cutting. A centrally located spot for your vacuum will make cleanup a routine, less onerous task.

If you already own tools, you'll have a ballpark idea of how much storage and worksurface will be needed. But if you're just getting started, do some research to find the overall size and footprint of benchtop tools you'd like. A fixed space, such as an existing room, might mean you'll need to reconsider some of your tool choices if they're too large for the area. Trying to cram too much equipment into a small space can create a workflow nightmare. Aside from tools, consider the other things you'll need in your shop. Hardware storage is important because there are standard items, such as nails, screws, nuts, and bolts, that you should keep on hand to avoid making constant trips to the hardware store. If the space is big enough, you may also want to store some materials, such as some common lumber, or at least have a place to keep useful scraps.

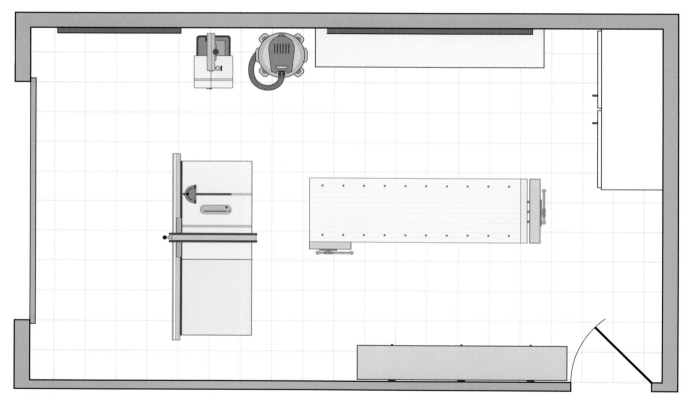

A single-bay garage shop affords many advantages, including easy access through the overhead door, generous room, a linear workflow, good dust and noise abatement, and excellent ventilation. In this example, the tablesaw is in line with the overhead door to allow efficient cutting of sheet goods and the workbench serves as an outfield table for large stock. This shop also has a wall between it and the other garage bays, which creates more potential storage and keeps the dust off of vehicles.

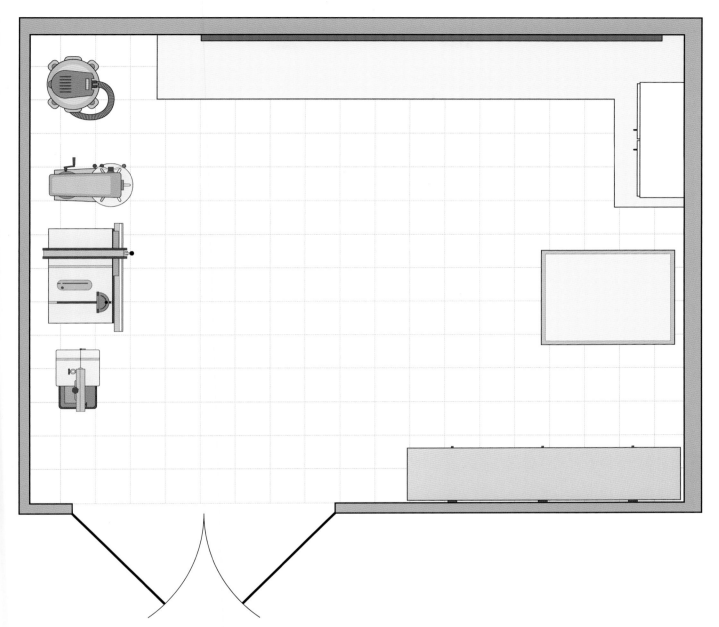

Basement shops are often located in a corner. Framed walls help contain dust and noise and provide the opportunity for more hanging storage. Bench or stationary tools on rolling stands give a small space more flexibility and ease cleanup. A long worksurface against a wall is a good spot for benchtop power tools and some assembly work. Pegboard above the worksurface provides quick access to often used tools. Double doors allow moving large materials and projects with ease.

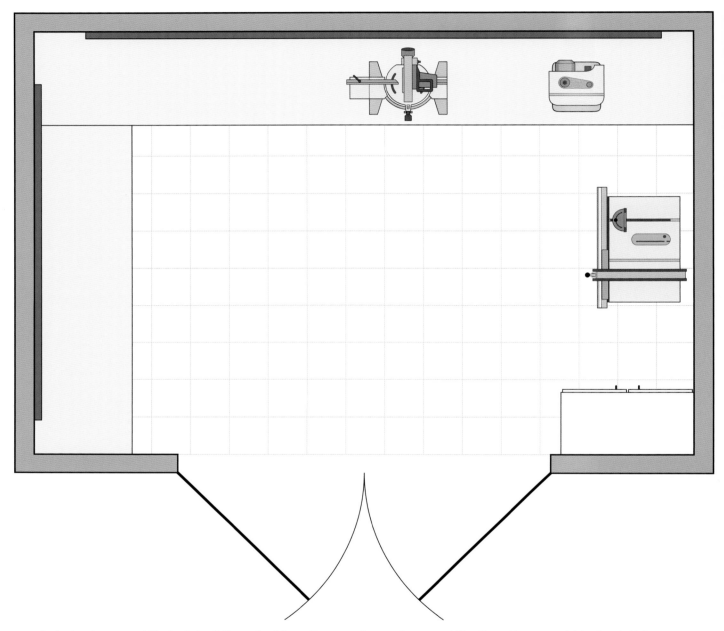

A shed makes a good "instant shop" if you don't have the space in your house and it's allowed in your neighborhood. Using the perimeter for the work areas and storage, and keeping the center floor area open, allows storage of other items, such as gardening tools and mowers, when not using the shop. The open areas under the counters are usable for drawers, shelving, and modular containers.

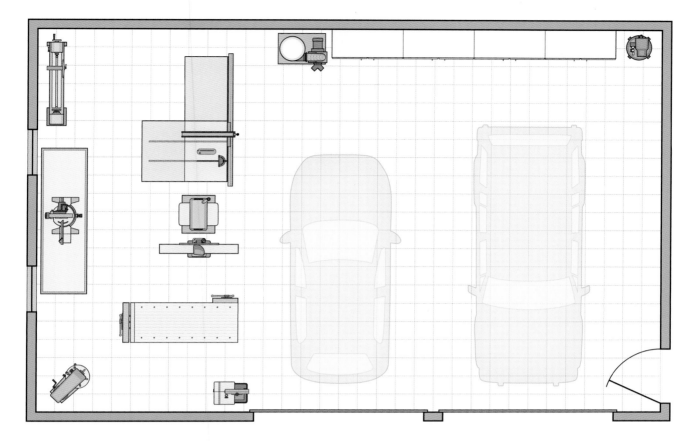

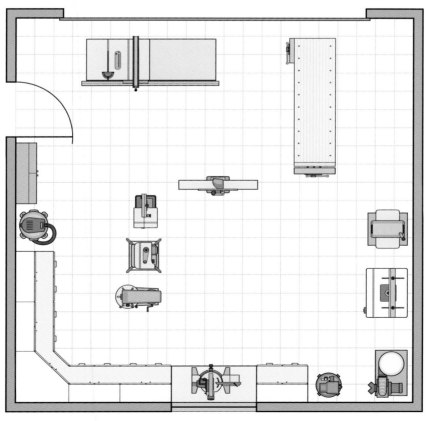

If you have the luxury of an extra stall or storage area in your garage, the workshop layout world is wide open—even if the square footage of the space is not large. Whichever stationary equipment and work stations you select, arrange them to create an efficient workflow.

Having enough light in a shop keeps you safe and helps prevent fatigue. A small shop doesn't need as many fixtures as this large shop, but it shows the importance of placing lights over work areas.

Lighting & Electrical Requirements

Good lighting and safe electrical service are not just nice to have; they're a requirement for any shop. A shop that's properly wired to support your tools' electrical needs reduces the risk of fire and can also extend the life of your tools. Being able to see clearly reduces fatigue and can even contribute to the quality of your work—fine, precise woodworking is hard to accomplish if you can't see. Of course, having enough illumination to work safely depends on factors such as the size of your shop, the ceiling height, the reflectivity of the walls and ceiling, and the type of bulbs and fixtures. Because of these factors, there's no one-size-fits-all formula, but there are some good starting points. Ultimately, you must be the judge of whether the illumination in your shop meets your needs.

Proper electrical service is more complicated, though, and unless you're well versed and skilled in electrical matters, you should leave all but basic upgrades and tasks to a licensed electrician. A good place to start thinking about electrical service is with some basic understanding of lighting.

This bandsaw uses a conventional point-source fixture with a screw-base LED lamp to illuminate the work.

Lighting

Most shops need at least overhead fixtures for area lighting. And when using some tools, such as bandsaws, lathes, and routers, a point-source light can provide visual modeling that makes it easier to see fine details.

Standard fluorescent shop fixtures (two 48-inch 40-watt lamps or the LED equivalent) provide the best all-purpose area lighting. They can be mounted to or in the ceiling directly over workbenches, stationary tools, and assembly areas for the most benefit. Alternatively, the fixtures can be mounted at regular intervals to provide even light throughout the shop. Depending on the size of your shop, start with a minimum number of fixtures and add more as needed—your shop should be bright enough so you don't have to strain to see. For example, an 8 × 10-foot area will typically require at least two

standard fixtures. However, if the walls and ceiling have low reflectivity or the ceiling is unusually high (more than 10 feet), additional lighting may be needed.

Fluorescent lights (both tube and screw-base) are rapidly being phased out and replaced by LED lamps. Recently, these fixtures have become much more affordable and have several significant advantages. Unlike fluorescent lamps, LEDs don't flicker and generally have better color balance characteristics that are more akin to natural daylight rather than the green- or blue-tinged light common with fluorescents. The lopsided color balance of fluorescent lamps can make it difficult to accurately see fine details and color, and causes eyestrain. LEDs are also highly efficient, which means they're more economical to run and

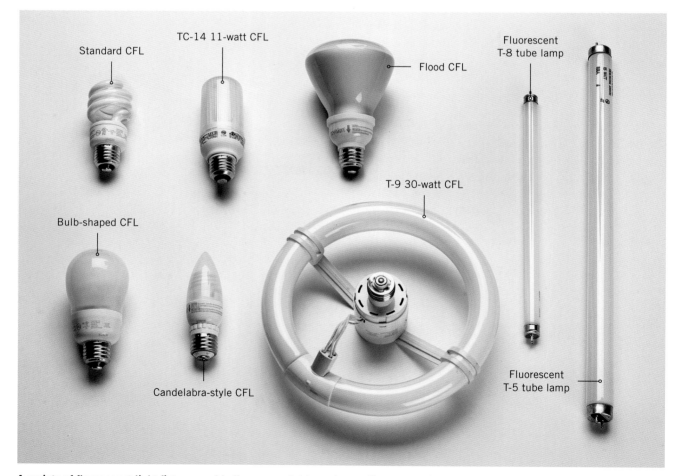

A variety of fluorescent light fixtures and bulbs are available and are still common for workshops. Those designed to screw into standard light fixture sockets are known as compact fluorescent lights (CFL). Although beginning to be replaced by LED fixtures and bulbs, fluorescents still offer advantages over standard incandescent lights, such as consuming much less electricity.

Screw-base LEDs have the same advantages as their strip-light counterparts, and they also run much cooler than incandescent and fluorescent bulbs.

If you can locate your shop in a space with windows, you'll find that the natural light is easier to live with during long shop sessions.

generate less heat than most other types of lighting. Unlike fluorescent lamps, LEDs achieve full brightness instantly. The long life cycle for many LED lamps—typically 25,000 hours or more—means they'll last for many years without needing to be replaced. So, the higher initial cost is more than offset by their long life. Screw-base LEDs, which are useful as point-source work lights, are also more rugged than standard incandescent bulbs and compact fluorescents, and, like incandescent lamps, they can be dimmed with suitable switches.

Natural light may not be as consistent in its brightness and color balance as artificial light sources, but it's the easiest on your eyes. Skylights and windows can provide warmth and soft, pleasing shadows for a less "clinical" work environment. Windows that face north deliver consistent, diffuse light throughout the day, but any window will work if you equip it with a translucent shade or screen.

Regardless of the light source you use, walls and ceilings that have been drywalled and painted white increase the efficiency of the light by reflecting rather than absorbing it. White walls also ease harshness by diffusing light for even distribution. If drywall isn't an option, you can use a white material such as foam-core board or melamine-coated hardboard as reflective surfaces in strategic places, such as over your workbench.

TERMS

- **Color temperature**, for practical purposes, refers to how the light in a room appears to your eyes, such as warm (red) or cool (blue).

- **Incandescent lamps** use a wire filament that glows brightly at a high temperature when an electric current is applied.

- **Fluorescent lamps** are highly efficient light sources that use mercury-vapor gas and phosphors to produce a glow when an electric current is applied.

- **LED** stands for light-emitting diode. It is perhaps the "best" light source in terms of cost, life span, and efficiency.

- **Lumens** is a quantitative measurement of how bright a light source is: more lumens equals more light.

Electrical Service

Determining the right amount of electrical service for your shop is a bit of a chicken-or-egg discussion. The tools you use will determine the level of electrical service you need, and the electrical service you currently have will set the safe limit on the number and types of tools you can use.

You may already have adequate service in your shop, but if you have visions of a shop with more and larger tools, you'll most likely need to increase the scope of service. That's not something you should attempt yourself unless you are quite skilled; in most cases, it's a job for a licensed electrician. And if you're in the process of designing or building a new shop area, it pays to get advice from an electrician. Once you know the types of tools you'll use and where they'll be used, an electrician can help you determine the service required and its placement. Whether you do electrical upgrades yourself or not, you should always be sure to get a permit for the work and have it inspected as required by code and your municipality.

If your main circuit breaker box is located not too far away from your shop and has empty circuit breaker positions, it's a fairly easy job to have an electrician run a few extra circuits to your shop area.

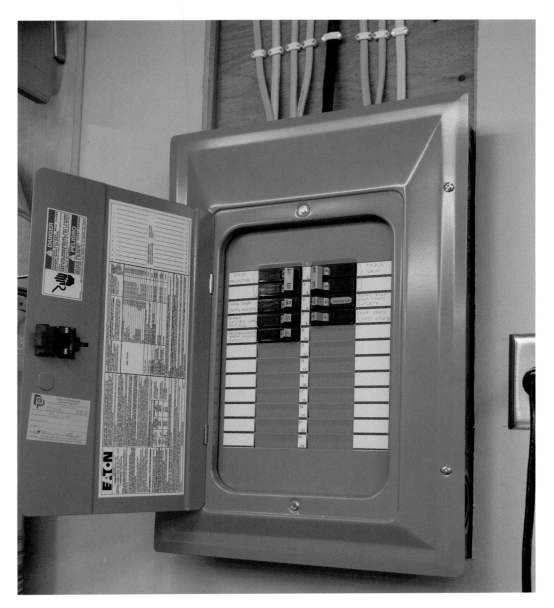

If your shop and main service panel are separated by significant distance or if the available empty slots are inadequate in the main, then you may need to have an electrician run a sub-panel to your shop site—a solution that may be most practical if your shop is in a detached garage or shed.

Residences have an electrical service panel (also called a load center) that divides power usage through circuit breakers. Most residential service panels range from 100- to 200-amp capacity. Higher-capacity service panels have more circuit-breaker stations and allow more electrical devices to be run at the same time, within the specified limits of the panel. (Some older homes may still have fuse boxes, but most have been modernized.) The job of the circuit breaker is to automatically disconnect the power if the electrical load being placed on it exceeds its rating. A breaker can be reset once it's determined that the cause of it tripping isn't a systemic problem, such as a defective breaker or loose wiring. A tripped breaker can be the result of several factors, such as a sudden electrical draw, a short circuit, or overheated wires. It's important to remember that if a breaker trips you should never try and override it by installing a larger one (this also applies to fuses) or try to lock it into the on position, which would create a serious fire risk.

Most 120-volt household lighting circuits are rated at a minimum of 15 amps using 14-gauge wire. Circuits that draw higher loads, such as kitchens and laundry rooms, are required by electrical code to use 20-amp breakers and to be wired with 12-gauge wire. Most shops also require at least that level of service and may also need 30- to 50-amp, 240-volt dedicated circuits to serve larger stationary tools, including tablesaws, jointers, planers, and large dust collectors. Trying to operate a workshop on standard 15-amp household lighting circuits will be very difficult, and you may quickly find you are tripping circuit breakers regularly, even when operating only portable power drills or power saws.

If your shop is close to your home's main service panel and it has open breaker stations, it may be fairly inexpensive to upgrade it with a few additional circuits for your shop. Most main service panels tend to be located in basements or garages, which conveniently are both common shop sites.

However, if there's too much distance between the main panel and the shop (for example, one is in the garage and the other is in the basement), a small satellite sub-panel might make more sense than running several independent circuits. It will also put control of your shop's electrical system within easy reach and make future upgrades easier. Electrical code dictates where service panels can be installed and how far away from other utilities (gas and water lines, HVAC, etc.) they need to be. You will always need a permit and inspection for this sort of electrical work. National, state, and local codes are very specific and can vary, so that's another good reason to leave the work to a qualified electrician.

Of course, the size of the box and the number of circuits you need depend on the size of your shop and how many workstations and tools you have. One 20-amp circuit in a shop should serve no more than one quadraplex outlet, but that doesn't mean you can, or should, run four power tools simultaneously on that circuit. The four outlets are there mainly for convenience to reduce the need to constantly swap plugs. The number of amps each tool draws will determine how many you can run, and the combined total should not exceed the circuit's rating. (Power tools generally have the amperage rating, watts, voltage, and other information printed on their identification label.)

Identifying shop circuits—whether in your main panel or in a subpanel—will help keep you safe and save time if you need to resolve a problem, such as resetting a tripped breaker or shutting off a circuit.

An electrical tester like the one shown here can help you diagnose a problem with an outlet and check to make sure it is properly wired. A key label will tell you how to interpret the combination of colored neon lights that light up when the tester is plugged in.

It's a good practice to number or name the circuit breaker in the service panel and on each corresponding outlet box to make identification easy if a breaker trips. Surface-mounted steel conduit (GRC, galvanized rigid conduit; or EMT, electrical metallic tubing) and steel outlet boxes make it easy to run circuits and provide excellent protection against physical damage to the wire conductors. (The box connectors used to join conduit and outlet boxes must be compatible and code-compliant.) This method also simplifies moving outlet boxes if you decide to change your shop layout.

Only three-prong grounded receptacles should be used in a shop. Although many power tools have two-prong plugs, this does not eliminate the need for grounded circuits. Typically, in the United States, 120-volt wiring uses black or red hot-wire insulation, while the neutral is white and the ground is green or bare. If you need to replace an outlet, you'll want to be careful to match the colored wires to their correct corresponding positions on the receptacle. Also, outlets are rated for amperage, so depending on the applicable code, you may be required to use 20-amp-rated outlets for your shop.

A ground-fault circuit-interrupter (GFCI) receptacle has a built-in circuit breaker that trips almost instantaneous when short-circuited. It's required in wet areas such as bathrooms, as well as any below-grade or outdoor locations. Basement shops and garage shops will normally require GFCIs.

There are several types of 230/240-volt plugs and receptacles for various load ratings. Your shop tools may have several different shapes; the variation serves as a safety feature to ensure that you plug the tool into a circuit that has the correct voltage and amp rating. Shown above is a 20-amp 240/250-volt plug and outlet. It is very important that you not attempt to plug a 120-volt tool into this type of outlet. If you have tools that don't match the outlet shape, call an electrician for assistance.

If the circuit you're using is suitable, this type of heavy-duty extension cord makes it convenient to run more than one tool at a time, or to use them alternately without having to unplug and plug in constantly.

Building codes require the use of ground-fault circuit-interrupter (GFCI) outlets in many locations. If you have a sink in your shop and need a nearby outlet, for example, it should be a GFCI outlet. Similarly, most codes require GFCIs for any outlets installed below grade, such as in a basement, or in outdoor or outbuilding locations. This means that your shop outlets very likely must be GFCIs, and it's a good idea to install them in your shop even if not mandated.

This type of receptacle has a built-in breaker that will trip almost instantly to reduce the risk of electrical shock in the event of a short circuit. Things can get complicated with larger tools that require 240-volt service; they have a specific plug to support the amperage draw of the tool's motor. You should not change the plug to fit an existing receptacle, but rather ensure that the circuit's wiring and circuit breaker are a proper match for the tool. Bear in

mind that many newer 240-volt tools use a four-wire setup—two live wires, a neutral, and a ground.

Extension cords and power strips are shop staples, and choosing the right ones and using them properly will keep you and your shop safe and your power tools running properly. For shop use, you should almost always choose round-profile cords with three-prong plugs. Flat, two-wire cords are fine for lamps and table radios, but not for power tools, and especially not for heating appliances, such as portable space heaters. If there's any doubt about the specific size and safe maximum length of the extension cord you can use with a particular power tool, refer to the tool's instruction manual for advice. But there are some basic guidelines to follow:

- The cord's gauge should never be larger than the gauge of the circuit's wire. In other words, if the

circuit is wired with 12 gauge, the extension cord should be the same size or smaller (i.e., 14 or 16 gauge).

- The longer an extension cord is, the more the voltage will drop due to resistance. If the cord is too long, it can cause a power tool's performance to suffer and possibly damage or ruin it.

- It's never a good idea to gang extension cords of different gauge sizes together, particularly when running smaller to larger ones in the direction of the electrical flow.

- If the tool you're using has a grounded three-prong plug, always use a grounded three-wire extension cord. A "cheater plug" is not an acceptable workaround, and conversely, never remove the grounding pin on a three-prong plug to make the plug fit a two-prong outlet.

- When a cord becomes damaged (the insulation is cut or cracked, exposing bare wire) it should be discarded—it's cheaper to replace an extension cord than a house.

- In most cases, extension cords are not substitutes for proper wiring. If you're using an extension cord to supply power to a stationary tool, you should move the circuit so the receptacle is within reach of the tool's power cord. However, there are some tools that have very short power cords and require an extension. In these instances, you should refer to the tool's instruction manual to choose the correct length and gauge of extension.

Power strips are useful because they allow you to plug in several tools at once to eliminate the hassle of changing plugs when you switch tools. However, that's not to say you can run those tools at the same time—you're still limited by the capacity of the circuit. A power strip can be plugged directly into a receptacle or into an extension cord, provided the strip's wire gauge number is the same or less than the extension cord's.

Some power strips have a built-in circuit breaker to guard against an overload or a short circuit, although it's probably redundant if your shop is wired properly. There are also some models with surge protectors, which can help protect electronic equipment but aren't really needed for power tools. Look for power strips with three-prong outlets that can handle the amperage draw of portable power tools.

A power strip such as this with a built-in GFCI makes a convenient bench-top power source and can also be used for site work.

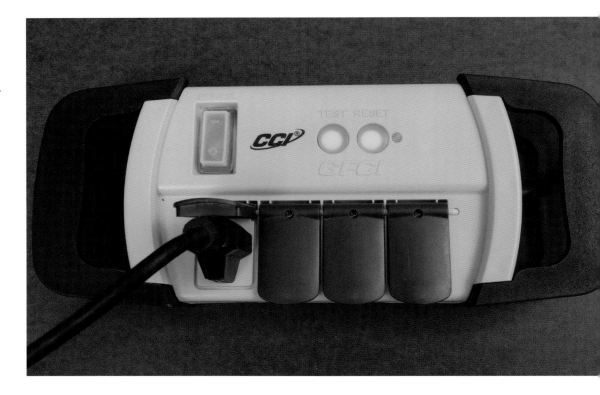

ESTIMATING POWER LOADS

The relationship between volts, watts, and amps can be expressed in a simple mathematical formula: Volts × Amps = Watts. This can be expressed in a number of variations:

- Watts = Volts × Amps

- Amps = Watts × Volts

- Volts = Watts × Amps

Let's imagine, for example, that a single 15-amp lighting circuit on a standard 120-volt circuit has the potential to supply as much as 1800 watts (15 amps × 120 volts). It is generally recommended, though, that you place no more than 80 percent of the total capacity on a given circuit. This means that you really should be demanding no more than 1440 watts at any one time.

That might seem like plenty, if you are doing nothing more than operating a handful of 100-watt light bulbs. But heating appliances and devices operating motors draw quite a lot of power. A space heater, for example, may draw 1100 or 1200 watts when it is operating at high temperature. And a simple power miter saw may draw as many as 1400 watts when it first pushes the blade up to speed. It's not hard, then, to understand why your lights might dim, or your circuit breaker might trip, when you start up your tablesaw.

The answer? Make sure your shop has at least three circuits and maybe more, and don't operate anything other than basic overhead lighting off standard 15-amp household circuits.

- **Volt** refers to the electrical potential of a circuit, tool, or light fixture.

- **Watt** is a unit measurement of electric power. This is normally the rating by which the power draw of tools, lights, and other fixtures are measured.

- **Ampere (or amp)** is a unit of electric current.

- **Service panel** is the device that divides the main electrical feed into circuits.

- **Circuit breaker** is an electrical switch in the service panel that automatically interrupts electrical flow in the case of an overload or a short circuit.

- **Wire gauge** is the numerical expression of the wire's size. Most 120-volt home wiring is either 14 or 12 gauge.

- **Receptacle/outlet** is the fixture that allows electrical equipment to be connected to the power supply.

- **Short circuit** is when an electrical current travels along an unintended path and has the potential to cause damage and physical harm.

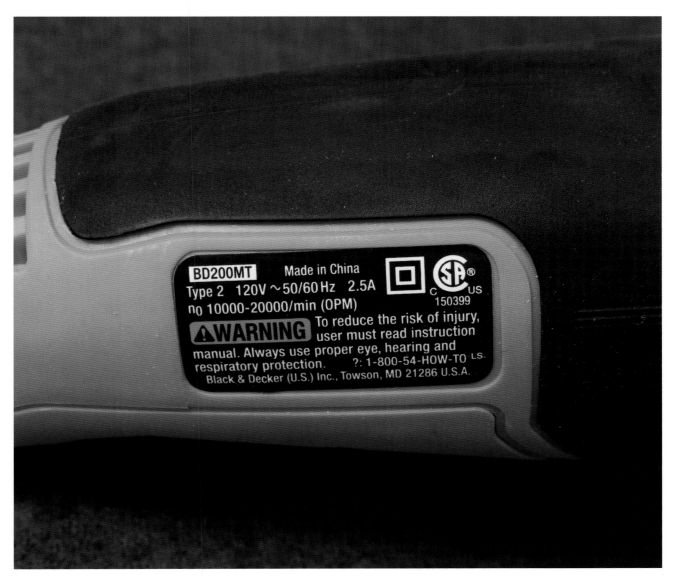

All power tools have an electrical specification label that will help you determine how many tools can be safely operated on a single circuit. This can also help you match up the proper extension cord to the tool if it is necessary to use one.

Whether a shop is large or small, it needs effective dust collection, particularly inside a house. Central collectors are made in suitable sizes for most shops.

Dust Collection & Ventilation

The romantic notion of a dusty shop strewn with wood shavings and scraps is often used in evocative photos meant to recall simpler times and a lost sense of craftsmanship. Aside from making pleasing calendar art, the reality is that such a shop is most likely inefficient and unhealthy. The tendency might be to skimp in this area, but maintaining a clean work environment is really the best approach because wood-shop litter can quickly compromise the quality of your work and your health.

Although you may be able to get away with somewhat looser cleanliness standards if your shop is in a garage or shed, there's not much leeway for basement shops or those in spare rooms. Wood dust and fumes in those locations can contaminate your entire house. So, choosing the right ventilation and dust-collection equipment is essential. And keep in mind that small shops can be more prone to higher concentrations of airborne dust simply because there's less air volume to "dilute" the dust. Even with effective ventilation and dust collection, you'll still want to wear an appropriate dust mask when sanding and a respirator when applying finishes that contain volatile organic compounds (VOCs).

Wood dust is a health hazard, not just an irritation, when it is inhaled. A particle mask (above) is an effective protective measure when working around sawdust and other airborne particulates. For maximum protection, especially when working with finishing products that contain solvents, wear a NIOSH-approved respirator or other protective device as indicated on the label of the product you are working with.

The type of dust collection you employ starts with the kinds of tools you use in your shop. While convenient and effective, sanders tend to generate fine dust that goes everywhere and gets into everything, including your lungs. Cutting tools such as tablesaws, bandsaws, and jigsaws make fine to coarse dust depending on the type of blade and material being cut. Dust-collection bags and vacuum ports on these tools can keep much of the dust off the floor and out of the air, but the finest dust will still escape and go airborne.

Portable power tools such as jigsaws, routers, and sanders can generate large amounts of dust, so a vacuum pickup port can be an important feature.

Air-Filtration Systems

An active air-filtration system helps remove airborne dust and is highly recommended for indoor shops. These are typically **ceiling-mounted, wall-mounted**, or **portable units** that circulate air at low speeds through a large replaceable filter. Some are able to filter all the air in a shop, while others are meant for more localized applications, such as above or alongside a workbench or a stationary tool. Most operate very quietly, so they'll cause little or no distraction when left to run continuously. This type of filtration is even more important as a second line of defense if it's difficult to integrate effective direct dust collection from a tool, such as a wood lathe or a sander without integral dust collection.

Light dust often goes airborne. An active air-filtration system will capture dust that gets past vacuums and dust collectors.

Shop fans and **exhaust fans** can be used to ensure a supply of fresh air and to direct fumes and airborne dust out of your shop. In high concentrations, volatile fumes can explode, and they can be toxic even in low concentrations. Common sources of volatile fumes include solvent-based paints, lacquer thinner, mineral spirits, and turpentine. And when it comes to exhausting volatile fumes, it's important to always use fans with totally enclosed fan-cooled (TEFC) motors to reduce the possibility of an explosion. Many of these motors are rated as "explosion proof."

Unlike a TEFC motor, an open-frame motor may produce an errant electrical spark that can cause fumes and even concentrated dust in the air to combust. With a TEFC motor, an external fan directs air over the motor housing to keep it cool, unlike an open-frame motor, which employs a fan blowing air through the motor. Of course, the size and installation of fans depend on the location. You'd need to have a suitable window or an external wall where you could cut an opening. And the bigger the shop, the larger the fan you'll need to effectively exhaust dust and fumes. Even if there's not a place for an exhaust fan, using a floor or wall-mounted fan to enhance your shop's comfort—particularly in hot weather—is something

to consider. An added bonus is that keeping the air moving in a shop helps prevent steel and cast-iron tools from rusting.

Shop vacuums and dust extractors are the most common collection devices for small home shops.

Vacuums

Vacuums are typically more affordable but less versatile than extractors. (Note that you should never operate a shop vacuum in an explosive environment. The motors in most shop vacuums have open frames and generate sparks.) They come in a range of canister sizes, will handle most cleanup chores, and can collect dust and small shavings from many portable power tools equipped with a dust-collection port. That includes most orbital and belt sanders, circulars saws, jigsaws, plate joiners, planers, and oscillating tools. Almost all vacuums come with a flexible hose and a selection of nozzles and cleaning attachments for floors, crevices, dusting, and so on. Depending on the vacuum's size and intended purpose, you'll find units that can be handheld or wall mounted, with others that are meant to be rolled around; they either have integral casters or separate caddies with wheels and casters.

The ubiquitous rolling wet-and-dry shop vac should be a part of every household cleaning equipment list, regardless of whether you have a workshop.

Most vacuums have a cartridge filter or a bag, or both, and many permit wet pickup to clean up nonvolatile liquid spills. Their usefulness is limited with most stationary tools, such as tablesaws, because they can't move the large air volume in a saw's cabinet quickly enough to effectively capture the dust being produced. However, they do work fairly well with most small- to medium-size bandsaws and smaller bench-top power tools, such as miter saws, sanders, and router tables.

When shopping for a vacuum, consider design details, such as its size, maneuverability, onboard storage, noise, ease of maintenance, and included accessories. Not all of these features are necessarily required or desirable, but they'll have an effect on how you perform your work. Despite its limitations, a shop vacuum provides the most bang for the buck and requires the least amount of floor space.

Dust Extractors

Although dust extractors look superficially like shop vacuums, they have added features that give them greater versatility, and they excel at collecting dust from portable power tools. They typically have a variable-power control that allows you to dial in the perfect amount of suction when collecting dust from portable tools such as orbital sanders, jigsaws, and routers. For example, being able to reduce the power to the extractor can prevent a pad sander from "sticking" to the work if there's too much suction. It can also eliminate or reduce the annoying high-pitched whistling noise that occurs with some tool/hose combinations.

Although a dust extractor may look like a standard shop vacuum, it has features that are specifically designed to make collecting dust from portable power tools efficient and convenient.

Dust extractors have variable speeds and a power-tool outlet that starts the vacuum when the tool is turned on.

This rectangular HEPA filter is housed above the dust extractor's collection canister so its efficiency isn't compromised by dust buildup.

Extractors can be remotely switched on and off by the tool in use via a built-in power outlet. When you turn on the tool, the vacuum turns on; when you power off, the vacuum keeps running for a short time to ensure all the dust is cleared out of the hose. Filtration is often located out of the path of the collected dust to help maintain maximum suction. In contrast, the filters on shop vacuums often extend close to the bottom of the canister, so they lose efficiency as debris builds up around them.

Extractors also employ high-efficiency particulate arresting (HEPA) filters and sometimes two layers of filtration—a bag and a HEPA filter—to remove very fine dust. (Note that some shop vacuums also accept HEPA filters.) When properly mounted, these filters are able to remove extremely fine dust and at nearly 100 percent efficiency. Unlike shop vacuums, extractors don't come with a lot of accessories. That's because they're primarily intended to be used as dust collectors for portable power tools rather than as all-purpose vacuums. If you need additional nozzles, wands, and hoses, you'll have to buy them separately.

HEPA filters on dust extractors remove even the finest dust produced by tools. Most standard shop vacuums don't provide this level of filtration.

A cyclone dust collector has two stages of separation, one for heavy debris and the other for fine dust. Compact units are available for smaller shops.

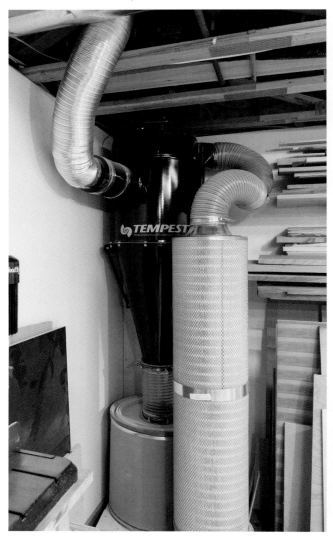 

Dust Collectors

Dust collectors take shop cleanliness to the next level. With stationary tools, such as contractor-style tablesaws and thickness planers that generate lots of waste in an unconfined space, there's really no substitute for a dust collector, because with these tools it's essential to move large volumes of air. Shop vacuums and dust extractors just can't do that.

There are basically two types of collectors: **single-stage** and **two-stage**. The smaller and often portable single-stage units are most often used with one tool at a time. They typically have a collection bag on the bottom and a filter bag on the top. Two-stage models, also called cyclone collectors, first separate larger dust and chips, which drop into a container, and then trap finer dust particles in a filter before the air is exhausted. When properly set up, two-stage

collectors are like a souped-up version of a whole-house vacuum, but unlike house vacuums, they move high volumes of air at a lower speed, while house and shop vacuums move relatively low volumes of air at high speeds.

Larger two-stage units are usually set up as a fixed collection point that serves multiple pickup locations for almost any shop tool as well as for general cleanup. Because of their size, the largest units are often installed outside of the shop. By installing fixed metal or plastic pipes and gates to regulate airflow, it's possible to create a system that offers more versatility and convenience than any other means of dust collection. (Static electricity can create an explosion hazard with systems that use plastic pipe, so they must be grounded with wires running through the pipe.)

A system with gates allows you to control suction at specific locations, so there's no need to move the unit to the tool. Opening a gate at one tool pickup point and closing the others in the system allows maximum suction at the open point. However, the more powerful the system, the more gates that can be left open to collect from multiple tools. That's useful if there's more than one person working with multiple tools in use. Although that's an unlikely scenario in a small shop, being able switch dust collection from one tool to another quickly is desirable in any shop. But if your space is limited and you don't need that level of functionality, it's best to stick with smaller single-stage roll-around and wall-mounted units.

In a central collection system, suction is maintained by opening and closing gates to individual tools.

Accessories

Having a dust-collecting device is only part of what's required. You'll also need a good selection of accessories to make cleanup convenient and efficient. Vacuum hoses and wands are usually included with shop vacuums, but not necessarily with dust extractors and dust collectors. A basic set of accessories for a shop vacuum, which will also work with a dust collector, includes a large and small floor nozzle, a crevice tool, a dusting brush, a wet pickup nozzle, and a few extra extension wands.

Because many shop vacuums can also double as a blower, a necked-down blower wand, which increases air velocity, can be useful for blowing dust and debris out of a garage or shed shop. The diameter of standard hoses and wands—nominally 1¼ or 2½ inches—determines the speed and volume of air being moved with a given vacuum. The smaller diameter hoses are most appropriate for collecting off portable power tools and for light cleanup, while larger hoses work well for general cleanup and dust collection from bench-top tools. Crush-proof expanding hoses can help reduce shop clutter and are more convenient and portable than standard hoses.

If the vacuum source is a dust collector, adaptors can be purchased or made to fit the collector's pipe size (4 inches is the most common).

With the addition of accessories, shop vacuums and dust extractors can be used as blowers and often for cleaning up spills.

Unfortunately, there's no standard size for vacuum connections, but a kit like this can make almost any hose fit to any tool.

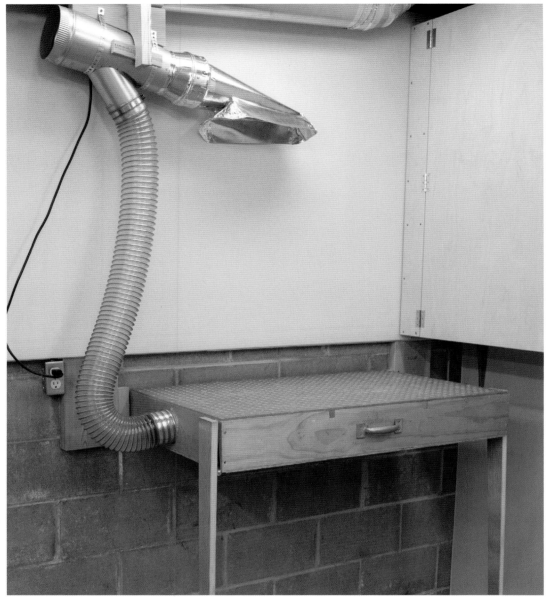

A downdraft sanding box is a good solution for dust pickup when a tool doesn't have a vacuum port, and it can be connected to any vacuum device.

A vacuum-assisted dustpan makes floor sweeping fast and convenient and reduces airborne dust. Vacuum ports on portable power tools aren't standardized, but an adaptor kit can allow you to collect from almost any tool using standard vacuum hoses.

Even if you have tools that aren't set up for dust collection, with a little ingenuity it's possible to make "proximity" dust pickup devices that can mitigate much of the dust problem. For example, a favorite shop project is the dust collection table that's effective when using pad sanders or when hand sanding small to medium-size workpieces. It's basically a shallow box with a pegboard top and a port for a shop vacuum. The size of the worksurface can vary depending on the size of the work you're doing and the power of the vacuum. The more powerful the

vacuum, the larger the worksurface can be. See the Benchtop Projects section for instructions on building this table.

Keeping your vacuum and its accessories stored in a convenient spot and well organized will make them more likely to be used. Although many shop vacuums have onboard storage, some of these arrangements can be clunky and get in the way of mobility, and they often don't really offer secure, convenient storage. A caddy or bin that's separate from the vacuum won't impede the unit's mobility, but still offers good access. However, some vacuums with separate caster/wheel sets may lend themselves to onboard storage. One simple feature of any caddy is to have a bottom that allows debris to fall through. A solid bottom will allow dust to collect and become a source of frustration.

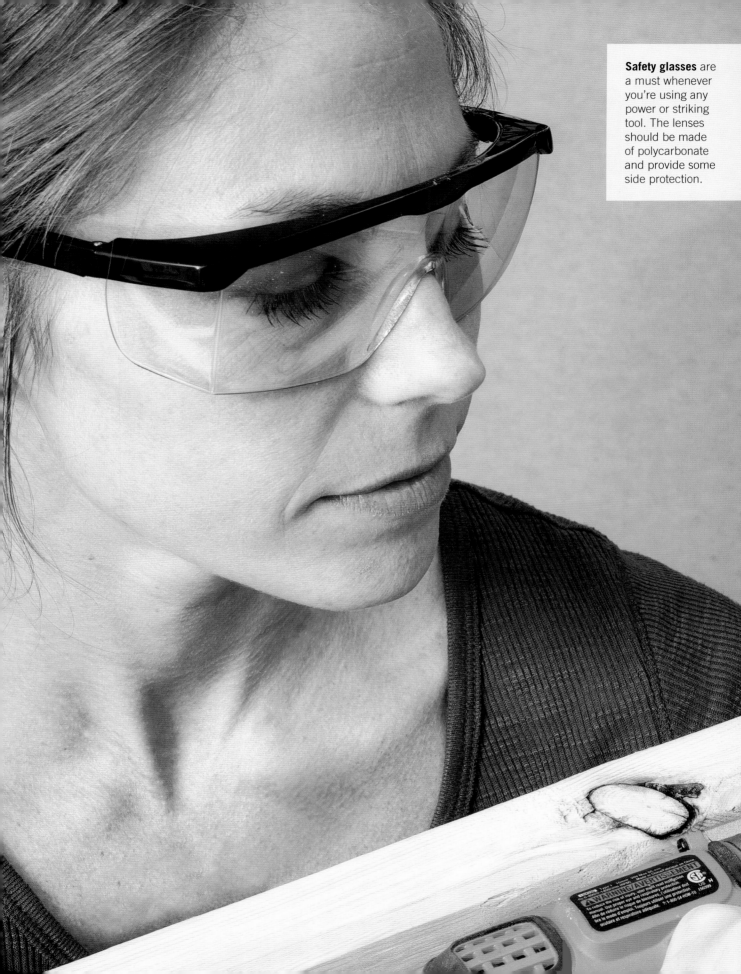

Safety glasses are a must whenever you're using any power or striking tool. The lenses should be made of polycarbonate and provide some side protection.

Personal Safety

The threat of personal injury in a workshop is not something anyone wants to think about, but taking care with your personal safety is essential to making your shop experience a pleasant and productive one. It really doesn't take that much effort to look after your own well-being, and unsafe practices and a hazardous shop environment can be distracting and have a negative effect on your work. Establishing good work habits and a patient attitude will ensure that you're actively staying safe, while the basic safety gear that protects your eyes, ears, lungs, and hands provides essential passive backup.

Eye Protection

It's a good idea to get into the habit of wearing safety glasses whenever you use power tools or do any finishing. Most tool manufacturers, for example, insist on it as a condition for using their tools—hand tools as well as power tools.

Safety glasses and **goggles** offer more protection than standard eyeglasses. Their lenses are made of polycarbonate, which is more impact resistant than acrylic, the standard material for corrective lenses. Look for the high-impact Z87+ rating on the frames. Even if your regular glasses have polycarbonate lenses, safety glasses typically have larger lenses that provide more coverage and often wrap around or have side shields for greater protection. Safety glasses with tinted lenses are available for outdoor use, and prescription safety glasses can be purchased at many optical shops.

Goggles add another layer of protection with a seal between the glasses frame and your face—a very real advantage when working with chemicals or in very dusty environments. And if you're grinding metal or doing wood turning, you should wear a full-face shield.

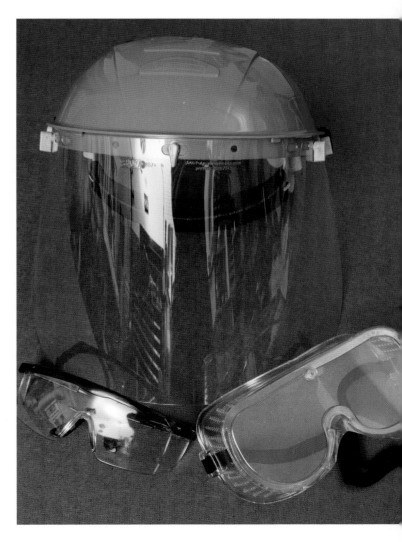

Various types of eye and face protection are made for different types of work. For instance, goggles are needed when working with some liquids and when there's a lot of debris in the air.

Hearing Protection

Power tools can literally be deafening—more than a few lifetime woodworkers have seen their hearing ruined after years of working with high-pitch tools while not protecting their hearing. Although some tools are louder than others, even short-term exposure to high-pitched motor noise can cause hearing loss. It's generally accepted that a sustained noise level above 85 decibels over time can cause permanent damage, and tools such as routers, shop vacuums, and circular saws can easily exceed that level.

There are basically two types of hearing protectors: **earplugs**, which fit into the ear canal, and **earmuffs**, which cover the entire ear. When used properly, they block about the same amount of noise—from about 15 to 30 decibels—but muffs block high frequencies better, while plugs are more effective at blocking low frequencies.

Earplugs are more convenient because of their small size, they're often very inexpensive, and it's easy to get them to seal tightly in the ear canal. The least expensive plugs are the disposable foam variety. The more durable and often more effective silicone earplugs are also available with a leash that keeps them conveniently draped around your neck.

Good earmuffs should have soft ear cushions that conform around your head snugly but comfortably to block sound. The headband should be padded, adjustable, and articulated to provide a good, comfortable fit. Some muffs even offer built-in sound canceling, a radio, and the option to plug in a personal listening device. In extremely noisy situations, such as around construction sites, both plugs and muffs can be used at the same time for maximum effect.

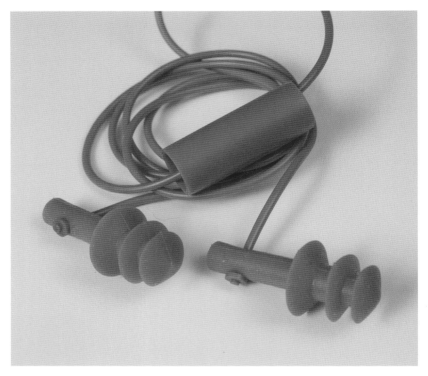

Earplugs are best for blocking low frequencies, but you can wear them with muffs to cover all the bases.

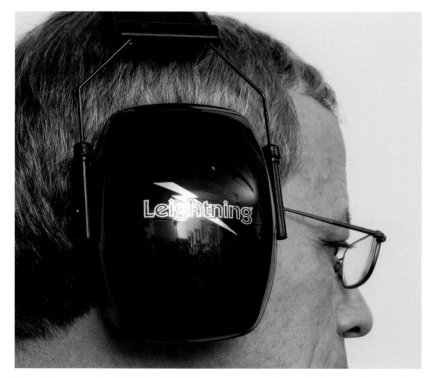

Earmuffs are good at blocking high-frequency sound, so they're your best choice when operating tools such as routers, sanders, and vacuums.

Breathing Protection

Protecting your lungs from dust and fumes is the job of **particulate (dust) masks** and **respirators** (gas masks), respectively. And just like hearing protectors, they need to fit snugly around both your mouth and your nose to function properly. A loose-fitting dust mask will let dust enter around the sides, and an ill-fitting or poorly adjusted respirator won't keep fumes out of your lungs.

Masks are often rated by the National Institute for Occupational Safety and Health (NIOSH) and the Mine Safety Health Administration (MSHA) for their function and effectiveness at filtering out fine particles. Good disposable dust masks have an adjustable nose clip and some also have a valve that improves comfort by expelling exhaled air. You'll want to be sure the mask doesn't interfere with your eye or ear protection and that it's comfortable to wear for extended periods.

If the dust collection on the tool you're using is highly effective, you may not need to wear a mask. But it's almost impossible to collect all airborne dust when using lathes, jigsaws, miter saws, most sanders, and a few other tools.

Finding the right respirator for your needs requires a little more attention. Most masks use two cartridges that are made to remove a variety of hazardous materials, such as VOCs, toxic dust, and acid gas. It's important to use the correct cartridges for your job and dispose of them when they're spent. If you can smell fumes through the mask, the cartridges need to be replaced. Respirators usually have a pre-filter to keep larger particles out of the cartridges, so you can also use it as a dust mask in a pinch. Disposable respirators are an option if you do a limited amount of finishing work. They'll last for several finishing sessions and cost less than masks that use replaceable cartridges.

Some respirators have an integrated full-face shield, which is a nice feature to have to keep mist and particles out of your eyes if you're spray painting. Of course, a mask's fit is key to its effectiveness and comfort, so a mask with a silicone face piece is usually your best bet. Silicone is more conforming and comfortable than the plastics used on cheaper masks.

A particulate dust mask should be worn in dusty environments, but it's not effective for filtering vapors from finishes.

The label on a respirator cartridge will provide information about its use. If you can smell fumes through the mask, it's time to replace the cartridges.

To filter volatile organic compounds (VOCs), often contained in finishing products, you should wear a respirator.

Face shields provide the protection you need when doing lathe work and some metalworking. However, they don't provide total protection, so you should also wear safety glasses.

Hand Protection

There are jobs when it makes sense to wear gloves, and there are times when you should never wear them. If you're working in close proximity to a moving blade or workpiece, you should take off the gloves for better dexterity. A blade can catch a glove and pull your hand into it, and that can cause a far more serious injury than might happen without gloves.

Specifically, avoid wearing gloves when using a tablesaw, a bandsaw, a lathe, a belt sander, a router, and similar tools. For that matter, avoid wearing loose-fitting clothing of any kind when working with power tools. There's too much chance they can get caught and pull you into the cutter.

But gloves should be worn to give your hands a needed break and save them from wear and tear when handling lumber, sanding, applying finishes, and doing cleanup chores.

Leather gloves afford the most protection when working with lumber, and rough stock in particular.

They'll guard against splinters and blisters, but they can get warm if worn for long periods.

Cloth and leather gloves provide more ventilation and can work for similar jobs. There are numerous brands of work gloves with hybrid synthetic and leather construction that have a trim fit and job-specific features—such as materials with extra traction for an enhanced grip, abrasion protection for extended life, and padding for vibration reduction.

Disposable nitrile exam gloves are handy to have around for applying water-based finishes and cleaning up liquid spills. But if you're using solvent-base finishes, you should use thicker nitrile gloves.

Some other useful gloves to have around the shop include knit cotton bricklayer's gloves with rubberized grips, Kevlar or stainless-steel chain-mail gloves that provide cut protection for woodcarving and close detail work with chisels, and fingerless gloves that protect your palm without compromising dexterity.

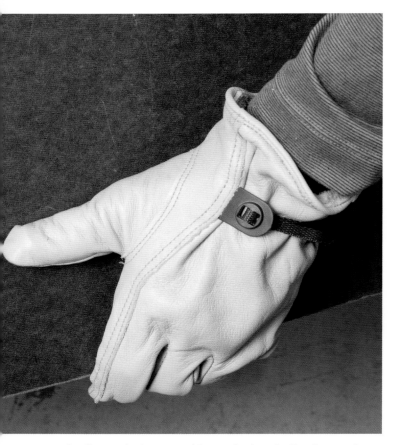

Leather work gloves provide excellent protection for carrying lumber products because they're virtually splinter proof.

Knit rubber-coated gloves are relatively cool to wear and they're useful for many shop applications, including finishing.

Fire Prevention

Beyond personal protection gear there are a number of items that should be in your shop to ensure safety. The most important of these is a multipurpose ABC fire extinguisher. This type of extinguisher uses dry chemicals that can fight fires caused by common combustibles (wood, paper, cloth), chemicals (liquid finishing products), and electrical equipment (motors, wiring). To be on the safe side, you should have more than one, storing them in easily accessible locations and not hidden behind other equipment.

A smoke detector or combination smoke detector/carbon monoxide (CO) alarm goes hand-in-glove with the fire extinguisher. A combination alarm makes the most sense if you have a furnace or heater in your shop, but this type of alarm also provides a more reliable and responsive system for detecting fires. Most alarms are battery operated, but some are hardwired with a battery backup, although the battery-only units offer the best installation flexibility.

The average life of an alarm is about seven years, and it must be replaced once it quits functioning. All alarms have an end-of-life and a low-battery warning, so you'll never be left unprotected. In some communities, smoke/CO detectors may be required in home shops by code, so check with your local code authority.

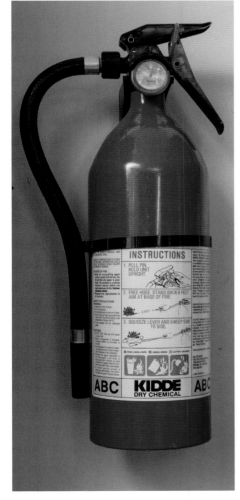

An ABC fire extinguisher will extinguish most types of fires. Be sure to mount it in an obvious, easy-to-reach location.

Shops are susceptible to fires, so a smoke/CO detector is essential and may be required by code in some communities. Models shown here include: (A) hard-wired CO detector; (B) ionizing smoke detector; (C) photoelectric smoke detector; (D) heat-activated fire detector.

First Aid

It's inevitable that you'll suffer an occasional self-inflicted cut or splinter, so it pays to be prepared with a first-aid kit. Most shop injuries are minor and can be dealt with on the spot. There's no need to go overboard—you won't be performing surgery—so a basic kit should be all you need. At minimum, the kit should include bandages in several shapes and sizes, gauze pads, sterile eye pads, alcohol pads, antiseptic or antibiotic ointment, bandage tape, small scissors, tweezers, exam gloves, cotton swabs, and over-the-counter pain medication.

In the case of a more serious injury, such as one that bleeds profusely or is quite deep, don't try to tend to it yourself—it's not a DIY project and requires the attention of a healthcare professional. What's really important is to remember that accidents most often happen for reasons such as losing focus, rushing through work, and becoming distracted or impatient. If an accident does happen—even a small one—take a break, gather your composure, and eat a light snack. For that matter, make a habit of taking regular breaks to help prevent mishaps.

But sometimes things just get out of control and you need to summon help, so keep your cell phone close at hand with the numbers of physicians, hospitals, urgent-care facilities, and 911 on speed dial.

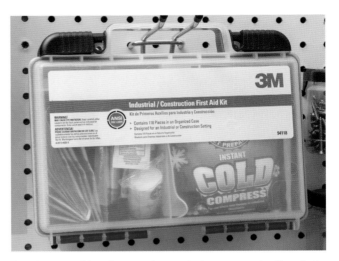

Should an accident happen, it pays to be prepared with a first-aid kit that's equipped specifically for shop mishaps.

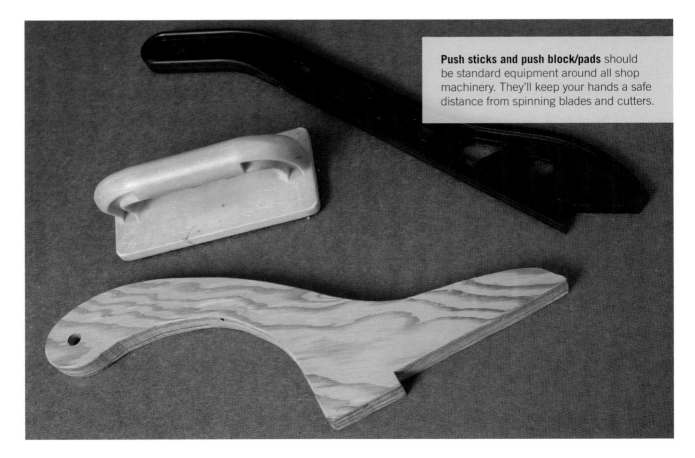

Push sticks and push block/pads should be standard equipment around all shop machinery. They'll keep your hands a safe distance from spinning blades and cutters.

Tool Safety Features

Removing accident-causing variables from your work routine is another way keep you out of trouble. There are some basic shop safety devices that should be standard equipment in your shop, on your workbench, and at stationary machines.

Push sticks or push pads are essential for guiding stock close to blades and bits on tablesaws, bandsaws, jointers, and router tables. They allow you to maintain steady pressure and direction on the workpiece while keeping your hands a safe distance from the cutter. Commercially made push sticks are available in a variety of shapes, or you can make your own out of wood or plastic (see the Benchtop Projects section of this book).

Attempting to hold or stabilize a workpiece with one hand while using a tool with the other is almost always an accident waiting to happen. **Bench dogs and stops** are most often associated with high-end cabinetmaker's benches to stabilize larger workpieces, but they're easy to make and install on any basic bench with a solid top. Simply use ¾-inch dowels and bore holes for them in the bench top. Then glue and screw small blocks on top of the dowels to prevent them from falling through the holes. When used together with clamps on the edge of the bench, they'll secure the work and keep it from moving when sawing, routing, and sanding.

Along the same lines as bench dogs, **bench vises** are generally used to secure smaller pieces and are a must-have fixture for all shops. Some are mounted to the edge of the bench top and others can be bolted to the top. They have an almost unlimited range of uses, including holding work for planing, drilling, routing, and gluing. Some edge-mounted vises with built-in dogs can also be used in conjunction with bench dogs to clamp or hold long workpieces. For this to work, the top of the vise must be level with the bench top and in line with the bench dog stations on the top.

Other devices that are usually included with stationary tools, such as **guards** and **miter gauge**, should be used when appropriate. When setting blade exposure on any tool, it should be the minimum amount possible while still being able to make a successful cut.

You may occasionally have visitors in your shop, and they need to be as aware of your shop safety rules as you are. Make it clear to anyone entering your shop while you're using a power tool that they should not interrupt in any way that might startle you. And if they enter unannounced, they should stand clear until you've completed the work and not try to assist you unless you request it.

Bench dogs aren't just a luxury for fancy workbenches; they can stabilize workpieces and keep them from unexpectedly sliding out from under a tool.

A bench vise holds workpieces so you don't have to. And it makes sense to have more than one for different types and sizes of work.

A cordless drill may be the most essential tool in the shop. It can bore holes, drive screws, and do many other jobs with the right accessories. A clutch behind the chuck lets you set the correct torque for driving screws.

Portable & Stationary Power Tools

Power tools are the workhorses that are meant to do the heavy lifting in a shop. With only modest skill and physical effort, you can pull off projects with speed and accuracy that would be difficult to achieve with hand tools. The three basic categories of power tools are **portable** (handheld), **benchtop**, and **stationary**. Although large stationary tools are the mainstay of major, full-size shops, portable and benchtop tools are your best choices in a small home shop.

The two portable tools that should be in every shop are a cordless drill and a saw (a jigsaw is the best all-around choice) because they're typically the most frequently used tools. Don't overlook hand tools, however, because they can complement power tools when you need to fine-tune your work or make a quick cut or adjustment.

Lithium-ion batteries have allowed cordless tools to become compact, lightweight, and powerful. These batteries can hold a charge for months without draining.

Power Tools

When you're ready to dive into a project, you'll want to reach for the power tools first. They'll allow you to rapidly, effortlessly, and accurately process material.

Cordless Drill

You'll find a cordless drill in almost every shop, and it should be the first power tool on your shopping list if you are outfitting a small workshop from scratch. The most popular models are in the 12- to 20-volt range. There are some models with higher and lower voltage, but for shop use, this range provides the best combination of power and portability. The tool's voltage rating is a rough indicator of its power, while the amp-hour rating of the battery is an approximation of how much work it can do before needing to be recharged. The higher the amp-hour number, the more work it can do. There are three features you should consider when choosing a drill:

- **Battery type.** Lithium-ion batteries, which are used on many cordless drills, are relatively compact, are lightweight, and can retain a charge over long periods. This makes them ideal for shop use if the tool's weight is important and it will be used infrequently.

- **Clutch.** A drill's clutch settings are meant to prevent stripping screw heads or overdriving by fine-tuning the torque delivered to the bit.

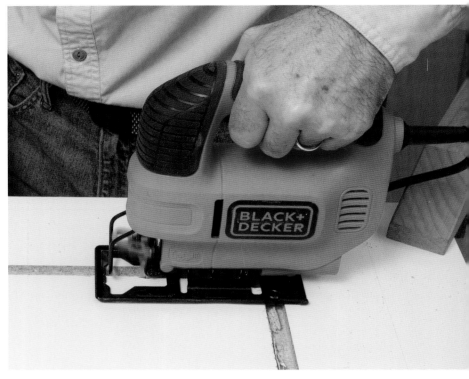

The jigsaw is as indispensable as a drill. It's a jack-of-all-trades saw that can make quick rough cuts, smooth precise cuts, and scroll cuts.

- **Speed settings.** A speed setting is useful when drilling into various materials—a high speed is good for wood and lower speeds are better for metal and plastic.

There are other drill variations designed for specialized work, such as hammer drills for boring in masonry, dedicated screwdrivers for assembly work, and impact drivers for deck building and other carpentry jobs.

Jigsaw

Cutting material is a basic operation for almost any project. And if you can have only one saw to tackle a multitude of tasks, it should be a jigsaw. With it, you can make freehand straight and curved cuts, precise straight cuts using guides, and inside cuts.

Most jigsaws accept a wide variety of blades and offer variable speeds that make it possible to cut a range of materials, including wood, metal, plastic, and more. Jigsaws are available in corded and cordless models, and in two styles—top handle and barrel grip. The amount of power is usually indicated by the motor amperage. But power isn't everything; how quickly and accurately a jigsaw cuts can be determined by whether it has variable orbital blade action (which increases cutting speed) and how well the blade is guided and supported. Depending on your needs and budget, look for features that offer convenience and enhance versatility, such as:

- A tilting base for making angle cuts

- A work light

- Keyless blade changing

- Dust blower and integral dust collection

Blades are available in two mounting styles—T-shank and universal—and both commonly fit most saws. And there's a blade to cut almost any material.

Jigsaw blades are made for a wide array of applications and materials, and come with tooth patterns that can cut quickly and precisely.

Circular Saw

The circular saw is another popular cutting tool commonly used for both woodworking and carpentry. Although it's not as versatile as the jigsaw, it packs more punch and can power through cuts much more quickly. It's typically used to cut materials such as construction lumber and plywood to rough dimensions, but with the right blade and a guide, it can make very precise straight cuts for fine woodworking projects.

Like other portable power tools, the circular saw is made in cordless and corded models. The most common blade sizes are 7¼ inches for corded saws and 6½, 5½, and 5⅜ inches for cordless saws. The cordless saws are offered in even smaller sizes and are used for doing trim work, cutting flooring materials, and working in tight quarters. Circular saws usually come with an inexpensive all-purpose carpentry blade, but you'll need a better blade for smoother cuts. There are a few general guidelines to keep in mind when blade shopping:

- Blades with more teeth will typically produce a finer cut.

- Carbide-tipped blades are more durable.

- Some blades are designed for cross-cut only (sawing across the grain) or ripping only (sawing with the grain).

- Thin-kerf (narrower) blades require less power to cut, so they're the best choice for cordless saws.

Although the circular saw is mainly a carpentry tool, it's also useful for accurately cutting plywood and cross-cutting oversize stock.

Pad Sander

Pad sanders come in several different varieties. The most common and useful types are **random-orbital**, **detail**, and **sheet** sanders. All of these sanders are designed to create a smooth surface that's ready to accept a finish such as stain, paint, or varnish. None of them is meant to aggressively remove stock like a belt sander, though.

The random-orbital sander is the best choice for most woodworking projects because it's easy to control and works quickly but not so much that it's aggressive on surfaces. It can remove stock relatively quickly with its eccentric, circular sanding motion.

Detail and sheet sanders have an orbital, vibrating action that works more slowly and is unlikely to cause any undulations in the worksurface.

Dust collection is an important feature on pad sanders because of the very fine dust they create. Random-orbital sanders use either hook-and-loop or self-adhesive paper with prepunched dust-collection holes. Most of them have a collection bag and a vacuum port. Detail and sheet sanders are more variable. Some sheet sanders have a vacuum pickup port, but they may require that you punch the collection holes in the sandpaper. Detail sanders often require sandpaper that's made specifically for that model. If you sand materials and surfaces other than just raw wood, you should select a sander with variable speeds.

Belt Sander

If removing a lot of stock quickly is your goal, then a belt sander is what you need. Standard belt sanders are identified by the size of belt they use, such as 3 × 18 inches, 3 × 21 inches, and 4 × 24 inches.

Of course, the larger the belt size, the heavier the sander becomes and the more difficult it is to control. For most woodworking projects made in the shop, the smaller sanders are more than adequate for the job. The larger tools are best used for carpentry projects.

Some of the tasks where a belt sander excels include leveling glued joints, renewing deteriorated stock, removing old finishes, and quickly sculpting the edges and corners of furniture projects. An important trick to remember is to always keep the sander moving to prevent it from digging in and forming craters.

Dust is a major problem with these tools, and although they all have collection bags, it's much better to hook them up to a vacuum or dust extractor. Sanding belts are available in grits from very coarse (60 grit) to very fine (400 grit) and in abrasives for a variety of applications.

Random-orbital sanders and detail sanders are both good for finish sanding. The random-orbital is faster and the detail sander can get into tight quarters.

The belt sander can remove stock faster than any other handheld power tool. It's good for stripping off old finishes and smoothing rough stock.

Router

Among all portable power tools, the router is perhaps the most versatile. With the right bits and accessories, you can make strong joints, form edges, trim laminate, carve letters, and shape decorative details. And there's a bit for every conceivable job—the range of bits is almost endless.

Routers are made in several sizes and configurations that are designed for specific tasks, depending on the size of the work and the location of the cut. **Fixed-base routers** are ideal for edge routing and for use in router tables. **Smaller routers** are usually limited to using bits with ¼-inch-diameter shanks, while **heavy-duty routers** accept ½-inch bits. **Plunge routers**, which use posts that guide the motor to make internal plunge cuts, are particularly well suited for tasks such as making mortises and anything that involves an inside cut, but they're equally adept at doing almost any job that a fixed-base router can do.

Router kits offer both fixed and plunge bases using the same motor, so you can have the best of both worlds. The addition of a router table can open up many creative possibilities. Properly set up, it will allow you to rout small and narrow workpieces, such as picture frames and furniture trim. There are many commercially available router tables, but making your own is a quick and easy shop project (see the Benchtop Projects section of this book).

A handheld plunge router is an extremely versatile woodworking tool that can make internal cuts, form edges, and reproduce workpieces precisely using templates.

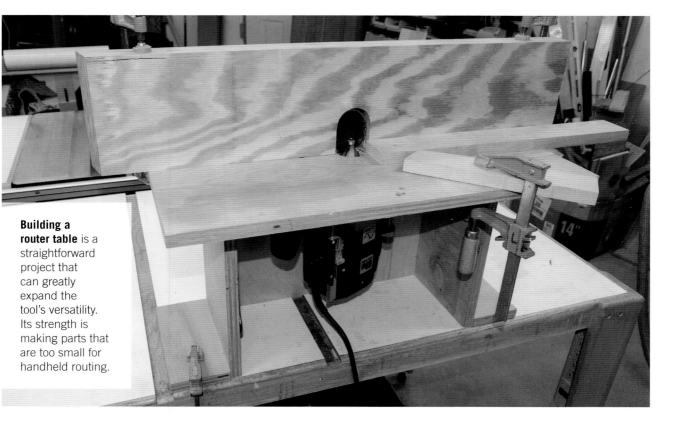

Building a router table is a straightforward project that can greatly expand the tool's versatility. Its strength is making parts that are too small for handheld routing.

A miter saw can cut precise angles and quickly cross-cut multiple parts, so it's well suited for making trim. The saw's capacity is determined by blade size and whether it has a slide mechanism. Most saws can also cut compound miters.

Miter Saw

A miter saw can do precision cross-cutting for many common woodworking and carpentry tasks. These saws are particularly useful for accurately cutting trim, molding, and framing materials, and for sizing long stock. But its most useful feature is the ability to easily make repeatable angle cuts, and many of these saws can be tilted laterally as well to cut compound angles.

A fixed back fence and stops that lock the motor and blade into position ensure consistent cuts. Miter saws come in several sizes, but those that use 10- and 12-inch blades are the most typical. Saws with larger blades let you cut thicker and wider stock but also require more bench space.

There are various types of saw designs with increasing levels of complexity, versatility, and capacity. The most **basic miter saw** makes a 90-degree vertical cut and can be adjusted to make left or right miter cuts. Stepping up, the **compound miter saw** also lets you tilt the blade off the vertical—some in one direction only, while others can tilt left or right (**dual compound miter saw**).

For increased cross-cut capacity, the **slide compound miter saw** has the motor mounted on rails that let it slide in and out perpendicular to the work. Unless you need the cross-cut capacity, a standard compound miter or dual-compound miter saw offers the most precision and will cost a bit less. There are a few cordless miter saws available, but these are best used as job-site saws; a corded saw is more appropriate for a shop. With a high-quality blade, miter saws can produce incredibly smooth cuts with little or no chipping.

Tablesaw

For many woodworkers, the tablesaw is an essential tool and is often considered to be the heart of the wood shop. There are few tools that are more versatile . . . or more hazardous if improperly used. You can rip, cross-cut, and resaw stock, and make many common woodworking joints, such as rabbets, dadoes, grooves, and tenons, with great precision. If the tablesaw is carefully set up, you can make small and intricate workpieces that would be difficult to pull off with almost any other tool. And like many other tools, tablesaws come in a variety of sizes that include **bench-top models**, **small portable units**, **contractor-style saws**, and large **stationary machines**.

For most small home shops, a tablesaw in the portable category with a folding stand makes the most sense, because it's the best compromise between size, power, and capacity. Except for a few small benchtop saws, the standard blade size is 10 inches. However, beyond the blade size, there's not much that's equivalent between small and large saws. The size of the table and the distance of the blade to maximum fence extension determines the ripping capacity of the saw, so the smaller the fence and extension, the less ripping capacity you'll have for sheet goods.

Smaller saws will generally have less powerful motors and aren't designed for continuous use. Fence accuracy and alignment are important because the fence must be locked parallel with the blade for a clean cut and to prevent dangerous kickback or binding. If a saw's fence doesn't consistently and accurately align with the blade, or if it's hard to adjust, that should be reason enough to pass on that saw.

All saws are equipped with a blade guard, anti-kickback pawls, and a splitter that should always be used when making through cuts. On some saws, these safety devices are convenient and easy to set up, while other saws seem to discourage you from using them; those saws should also be avoided.

Tablesaws create a lot of dust, and collection can be difficult even with saws that have well-designed built-in collection devices. That's something you should take into account when purchasing a vacuum or dust collector.

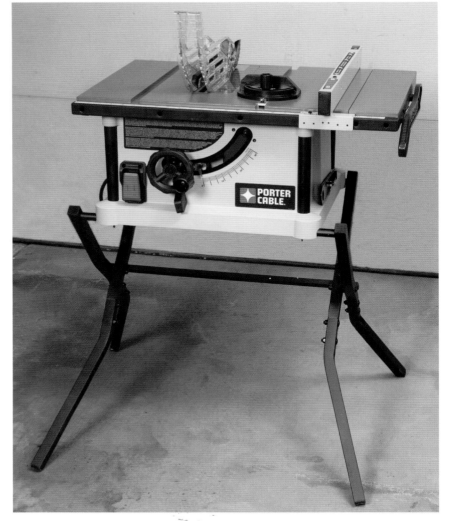

Tablesaws can rip or cross-cut equally well. They range in size from compact portable models like this to large stationary cabinet-shop saws. A saw with a 10-inch blade is the most suitable for general woodworking.

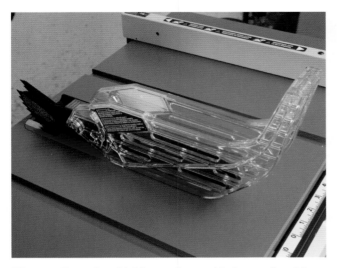

All currently produced tablesaws have a blade guard, a riving knife, and anti-kickback pawls that should be used whenever making through cuts.

Another important tablesaw safety feature is a paddle switch that must be pulled out to start the tool, and can be turned off by pressing it with your knee.

Oscillating Multi-Tool

The oscillating multi-tool's purpose can be hard to pin down because it can do so many things: sand, cut, carve, sculpt, grind, polish, scrape, and more. Multi-tools use a high-speed side-to-side reciprocating motion to do the work, and most feature variable speeds for compatibility with a variety of materials. The tool was originally designed for construction and home-improvement tasks but has gained popularity as a woodworking and crafting tool because of its ability to work in tight spaces and to cut or sand flush with surrounding surfaces. Because of this, it makes an excellent detail sander.

One of the tool's unique strengths is the ability to offset the angle of the tooling in relation to the grip, which is very useful in close quarters. Unlike drills and routers, there's no industry standard accessory-mounting system for this tool, so in some cases you're limited to the accessories sold by the tool's manufacturer. However, there are a few models that accept more than one mounting system, and adapters are available.

Tool-less accessory mounting is becoming more common, which makes setting up the tool much faster. Perhaps the most useful multi-tool accessories for woodworking are hook-and-loop sanding heads, thin-kerf saws, and scraper blades.

Grinders

Although **bench grinders** and **angle grinders** are primarily considered metalworking tools, they do have a place in a home shop and even a wood shop. A bench grinder can be used to sharpen chisels, screwdrivers, drill bits, and even lawn mower blades—but it's best used for smaller-scale work. And with a buffing wheel you can polish items and remove rust using buffing compounds. A 6-inch bench grinder with a coarse and a fine wheel is all that you'll need for a home shop.

Handheld angle grinders are useful for some of the same tasks as a bench grinder, but its portability is really about taking on bigger jobs. Unlike bench grinders, which use the edge of the wheel to do the work, angle grinders use the face of the wheel, so with the right accessories you can tackle heavy-duty tasks, such as sanding and stripping paint on large surfaces. And if welding is a skill you'd like to pursue, an angle grinder is essential for grinding, smoothing, and cleaning up welds.

Oscillating multi-tools are a favorite of trim carpenters but have found their way into the wood shop. They accept many types of cutting and sanding tools that can be turned off-center to fit into tight spaces.

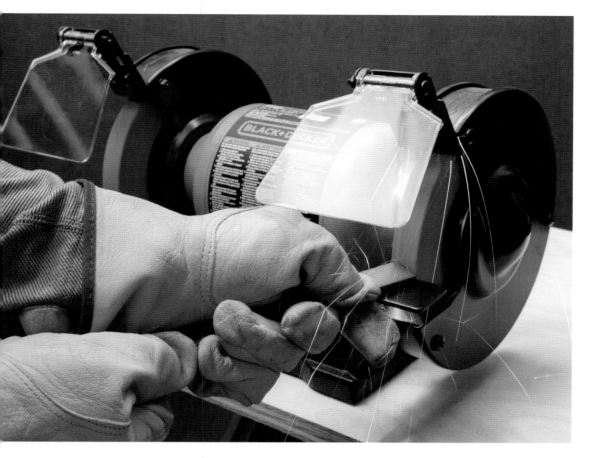

A bench grinder is useful for metalworking and crafts, and its ability to quickly sharpen chisels, screwdrivers, and plane irons shouldn't be overlooked.

Although it's primarily a metalworking tool, the angle grinder is an all-around performer that can be used for masonry work and for extremely fast sanding.

The bandsaw is a favorite of furniture makers and wood turners. It's great for making fine joinery, for scrolling, and for resawing thick stock.

The primary job of a jointer is to create two perfectly flat perpendicular surfaces. A jointer is not an essential tool, but if you're serious about woodworking, it should be on your wish list.

Other Power Tools

Finding space in a small shop for benchtop and stationary tools is always a challenge, but the **jointer** and **bandsaw** are a couple of tools that can help take your woodworking from basic to advanced.

If your projects are more crafts oriented, such as jewelry boxes and serving trays, small benchtop tools may serve your needs. But if you'd like to make full-size furniture, you'll need at least a 6-inch jointer and a 14-inch bandsaw. A jointer will produce perfectly flat and perpendicular stock surfaces, which are essential to making furniture joints that fit together

well. (Producing uniform stock thickness and width can be done with a tablesaw, a bandsaw, or most ideally with a thickness planer.)

The bandsaw can make perfect straight cuts, long inside cuts, and curves, and can be used to resaw wide stock. Blades are the key: they can be very narrow or wide, and, depending on the blade's tooth count, provide coarse or fine cutting. Narrow high TPI (teeth-per-inch) blades are used for fine work and scrolling, and wide low TPI blades are for resawing and fast cutting. And a bandsaw can take you in new creative directions. If wood turning is something that interests you, a bandsaw and a lathe are the only stationary power tools you'll need. Together, they can create a tiny pocket shop that fits tightly against a garage wall.

There are many unsung shop heroes (tools you didn't know you needed), but perhaps one of the most unlikely is the electric **glue gun**. It's generally regarded as a tool for crafting, but it's actually quite useful for woodworkers. An obvious application is for tacking or holding workpieces in place before making more permanent attachments. But it really shines when used for making prototypes, mockups, and models. Before committing expensive materials to a woodworking project, it's a good idea to use scraps, cardboard, or the like to test whether your two-dimensional plans will work in three dimensions. The almost instant set time of hot glue makes prototyping practical and can save time by helping you avoid design mistakes.

Glue guns are ideal for quickly fastening parts when strength isn't a primary consideration, and they're particularly well suited for crafts and model making.

Although it may not be an obvious choice as a basic tool, a pneumatic brad nailer is one you won't want to give up once you've tried it. Its ability to quickly and securely fasten any wood product makes it the number one time-saver in the shop.

Essential Hand Tools

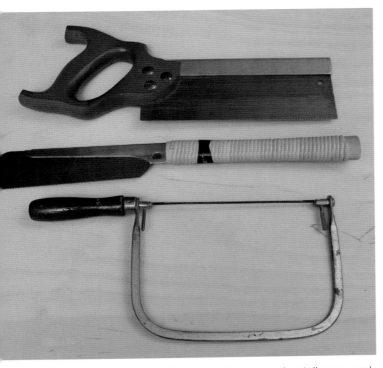

Handsaws such as pull saws, coping saws, dovetail saws, and carpentry saws have specialized uses that power saws can't always perform.

Hand planes are made in a number of sizes and for general purposes, such as smoothing surfaces and edges, and for specific jobs, such as forming rabbets.

Utility knives are workshop essentials that are used for many jobs, from cutting twine to marking joints to trimming veneer.

Screwdrivers are most commonly made in slotted, Phillips, and Robertson (square drive) versions.

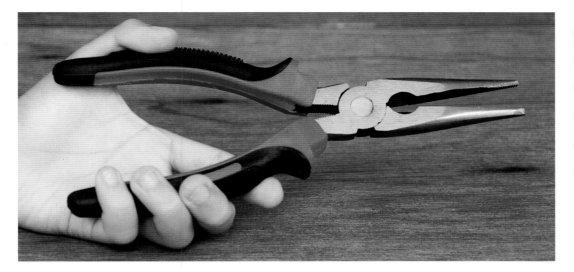

Pliers as a general tool category are essential for holding parts, cutting and bending wire, and pulling small fasteners. They are available in many different configurations.

Hammers are striking tools for driving brads and nails and tapping parts into alignment.

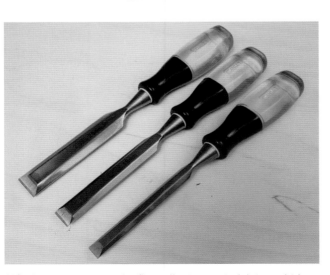

Chisels allow you to make fine adjustments to joints and trim small parts.

Tape measures, rulers, combination squares, and other **measuring tools** are standard equipment in every shop. **Pencils** and **permanent markers** are available in many styles and colors for various uses.

Woodworking Adhesives

Carpenter's yellow wood glue (aliphatic resin emulsion) is for indoor use, and there are also water-resistant types for outdoor use. These glues have a long open time and excellent strength in close-fitting joints. It's the best all-around glue for most woodworking projects.

Polyurethane glue can be used to bond wood, metal, plastic, glass, and other materials. It has excellent water resistance, good strength, and a fast cure time, and requires clamping because it expands as it cures.

Epoxy glue is a high-strength, two-part adhesive with structural (gap-filling) qualities. Cure times vary from fast to slow depending on the formulation and intended application.

Cyanoacrylate "instant glue" grabs on contact and cures very quickly. It bonds to most materials and is a good choice for repairs, crafts, and wood turning.

Hide glue is a traditional adhesive with good strength that's easily repaired and often used to make musical instruments.

Hot glue sticks fit in electric glue guns and are best used for crafts and temporary bonding.

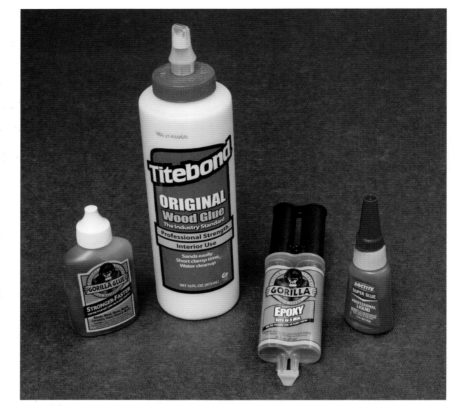

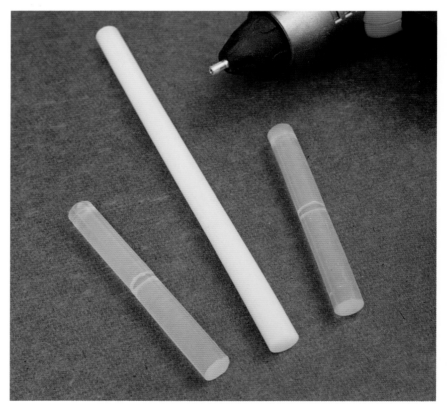

Woodworking Hardware & Fasteners

Dowels provide a simple hidden joinery solution that can be done with an inexpensive jig and a drill. **T-nuts**, **threaded inserts**, and other **knock-down fasteners** are useful for making sturdy plywood furniture and woodworking jigs and fixtures. **Plate-joining biscuits** serve the same function as dowels but require a specialized power tool, which offers the advantage of speed and perfect alignment.

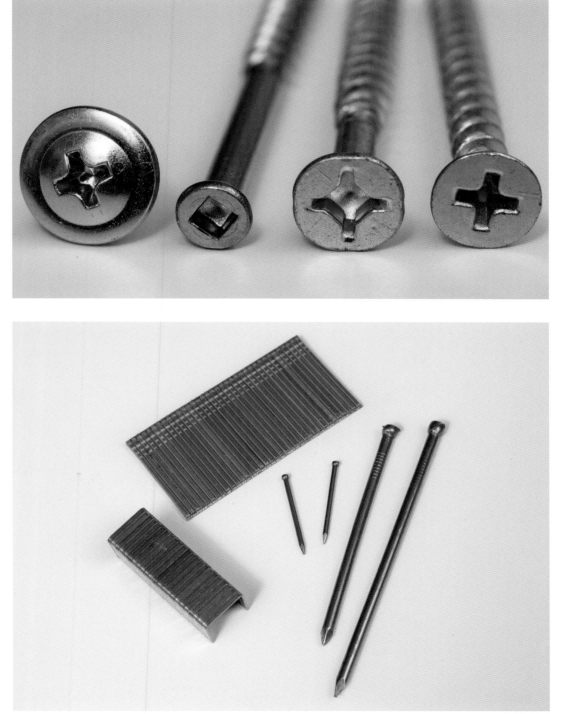

Screws, nuts, and bolts are the most common fasteners used in woodworking, and the types are almost infinitely varied and specialized. Phillips screws are the most commonly used type, but the square drive (Robertson) screw is rapidly gaining favor, because it's less prone to slippage (cam-out) when being tightened.

Nails and brads are not just for carpentry. They have an important role to play in cabinetmaking, and small pneumatic nail and pin guns are being used for furniture making too.

2x4 WORKBENCH

60"

30"

G.1

B

D

B

A

F

F

F

E

C

H, SHELF 2x4x18"

GLUE AND DBL FRAME MEMBER

LEGS ARE GLUED AND NAILED TOGETHER

SCREWS DRIVEN INTO INSIDE CORNERS

14-1/4"

54"

C

D

35" TO PEDESTAL TOP

TOP

60"

30"

LEG / CORNER DETAIL

3"

5"

3-1/2"

D

C

A

B

D

C

2x4 CUTTING DIAGRAM FOR FRAME/LEGS (2)

A 54"   B 23"   C 30½"   C 30½"   D 34"
D 34"   A 54"   B 23"   B 23"   C 30½"   C 30½"   C 30½"

(2x4 = 1-1/2 x 3-1/2" ACTUAL)

A 2 TOP FRAME FRONT/BACK .... 2x4 x 54"
B 3 TOP FRAME, SIDES/MIDDLE ...... 2x4 x 23"
C 8 LEGS, SHORT SECTIONS .... 2x4 x 30-1/2"
D 4 LEGS, LONG SECTIONS .... 2x4 x 34"
E 2 SHELF FRAME, FRONT/BACK ...... 2x4 x 18"
F 3 SHELF FRAME, SIDES/MIDDLE .... 2x4 x 20"
G 1 TOP, MDF .... 3/4 x 30 x 60"
H 1 SHELF, MDF .... 3/4 x 23 x 18"
J 1 TOP COVER, HARDBOARD .... 1/8 x 30 x 60"

Basic Woodworking Methods

Entire books have been written about woodworking, and about specific methods of joinery, so it is beyond the scope of this book to give comprehensive information on woodworking as a craft. Instead, this final chapter will give an overview of woodworking in a small shop and some tips for getting good results with your projects.

Behind every successful woodworking project there's a logical progression of steps and appropriate techniques that should be followed. Although they may not be the same for every project, there are many common elements:

- First you start with a drawing and/or prototype to nail down the concept.

- Then you need to create a materials and cut list and gather materials.

- Once that's done, determine which cuts to make first depending on the size of the part and the number of repetitive cuts. Make all the cuts of the same dimension at the same time so there's no need to repeat a tool setup. Cut all parts.

- After cutting the parts, label them and lay out the joinery in pencil. When making joints, cut the "female" parts first and then the "male" parts to fit. You'll want to use scraps to make practice joints before committing to actual workpieces.

- Always do a "dry run" before gluing parts together to make sure they fit, which also provides a sense of how you'll need to stage and sequence the assembly.

- Assemble the project with the chosen fasteners, and glue, if the plans call for it.

Joinery

There are just a few basic joints used in woodworking and several more refined and complex types that are variations that add strength and/or aesthetic appeal. The kind of joints you use and how you fasten them depends on the type of work at hand, but the basic principle for all joinery is the same—to form a mechanical connection between workpieces in a manner that's strong and appropriate for the project. There are no hard-and-fast rules for what's appropriate, but for simple carpentry, joints tend to be simple; cabinets have a combination of simple and more refined joinery; and furniture is typically the most complex when it comes to joinery techniques.

Butt joints are the easiest joints to make, and, as the name implies, they're simple square-cut edges butted together. A butt joint's mechanical attachment can be made with glue, screws, pocket screws, dowels, nails, plate-joining biscuits, or knock-down fasteners. Butt joints are commonly used in carpentry, cabinet cases, and knock-down cabinets and furniture.

Beyond butt joints, there are three simple joints that every woodworker should know how to make.

Grooves are cuts or joints that follow the same direction as the wood grain and are used to position and capture another workpiece, such as structural members in cabinets, shelving, and drawer bottoms. **Dadoes** are mechanically the same as grooves, but they run perpendicular to the grain and serve many of the same functions as grooves. **Rabbets** are two-sided cuts on the edge of stock and are often used to position cabinet backs, cabinet face frames, and drawer fronts.

There are also variations of the three basic joints that are used to refine the structure or appearance of projects. **Stop cuts** start on one edge of the stock, or between the edges, and terminate before meeting the opposite edge or edges. These can be dadoes, grooves, or rabbets and are often used to hide an exposed joint that might be potentially unattractive, such as a shelf-supporting dado on the front of a bookcase. An **inside (internal) stop cut** can also be a through cut. They're used for purposes such as creating access (drawer finger pulls) and for decorative jigsaw patterns, or for complex joinery, such as the mortise for a through mortise-and-tenon joint.

There's nothing simpler than a butt joint fastened with screws. You only need a saw and a drill/driver to pull it off.

If you don't like seeing exposed screws, plugging them is easy with a drill and a plug cutter. Just counterbore the screw holes and glue in a plug.

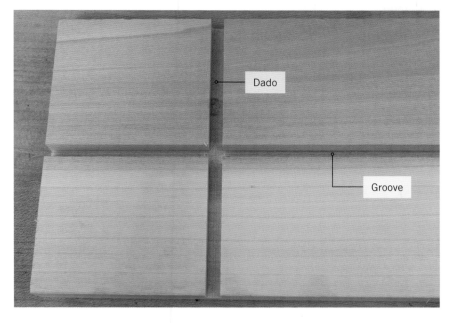

Dadoes run perpendicular to the grain and grooves run with the grain. A combination blade on a tablesaw will cut well in both directions, but specialized dado and rip blades shouldn't be used interchangeably.

Dado

Groove

Rabbets are two-sided cuts that typically run along the edge of the workpiece. A router used with a ball-bearing piloted bit is a fast and precise way to cut the joint.

Using a plunge router to make stopped grooves and dadoes is a basic operation in many cabinetmaking projects to hide the entry and exit points of the joint.

Using Tools

Safe work practices should always be exercised when using a tablesaw or router, the workhorses in most shops. A tablesaw can be particularly dangerous if not used properly because of its exposed blade and powerful motor. When making a through cut, always use the supplied guard and never make a freehand or unguided cut—you must use a fence or a miter gauge or other cutoff device.

Never stand directly behind the blade; if the workpiece binds in the blade, the stock can be thrown back with extreme force. Elevate the blade only as much as needed to cut through the stock—about ¼ inch

above the top of the stock. Never start the saw with the stock pushed against the blade and always use a push stick when ripping narrow stock against the fence.

Routers have their own set of rules, the most important being feed direction. When using a handheld router on the edge of a workpiece, guide the tool from left to right. But when the router is mounted upside down in a table, it's just the opposite—move the stock from right to left against the cutter. Going in the wrong direction when hand holding the router will cause it to "climb," or the stock to kick back if you're working on a router table.

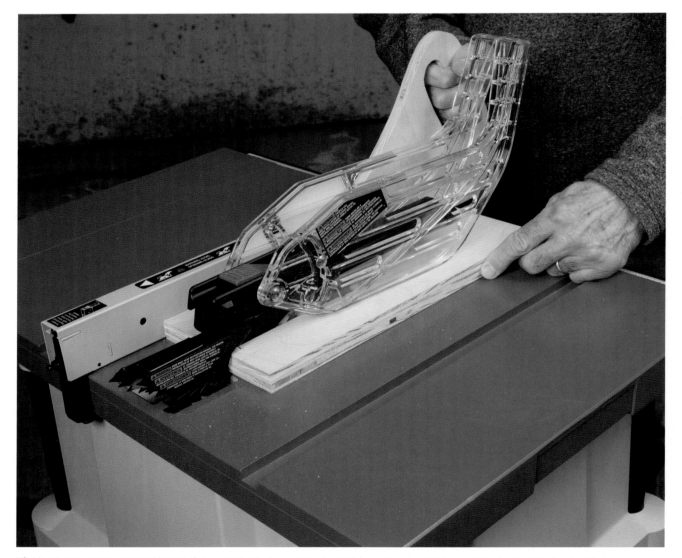

Kickback can occur on a tablesaw if the stock binds or gets skewed between the blade and the fence; that's why it's important to use the supplied guard with the riving knife and anti-kickback pawls. Of course, the guard also keeps your fingers clear of the blade.

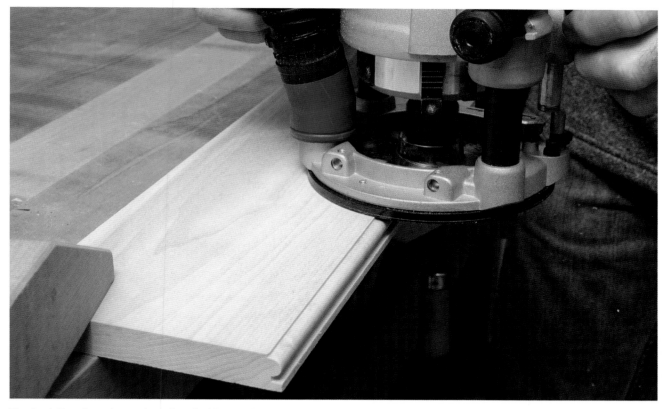

The feed direction when using a handheld router is almost always left to right. Routing in the wrong direction can cause the bit to grab the stock, which has the potential to pull the tool out of your hands.

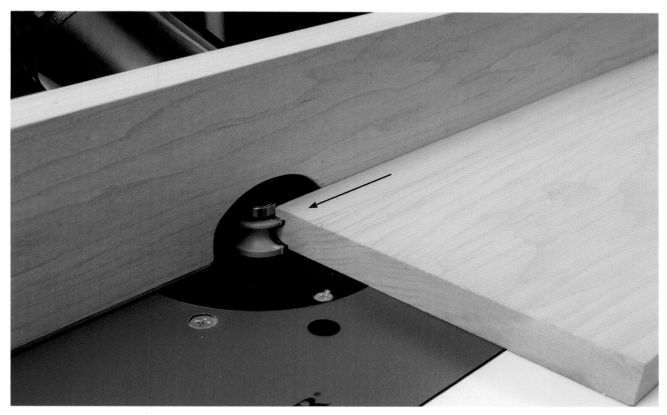

On a router table the feed direction is right to left. If you feed in the wrong direction, and you're not using a push stick or push block, your fingers will be at risk.

Plunge cuts can be made with a fixed-base router by tipping the running tool into the work, but it's much better to invest in a plunge router if you intend to make these sorts of cuts. Medium and large routers always need to be controlled with two hands, while small trim routers are meant for one-handed operations.

Make cuts no more than ¼ inch deep in a single pass. Deeper cuts may cause the router to get away from you and can also compromise the cut quality. When using any power tool, use eye, ear, and breathing protection, and avoid wearing loose-fitting clothing. Do not start a router when its bit is in contact with the stock. First turn on the router, and then move it slowly and smoothly into the work.

Rabbets, dadoes, and grooves can be cut with a variety of tools, but a tablesaw and router are the two most practical choices that can quickly produce the most accurate results. (Although it's also possible to cut these joints with a circular saw, it's not as easy or as precise.)

Not all tablesaw blades are the same. There are dedicated blades for ripping and cross-cutting, as well as combination blades, which are good all-around performers. To make the basic joints on a tablesaw, you can either use a dado blade or make multiple passes with a standard combination blade.

Dado blades can't be used on all tablesaws because the saw's arbor must have the capacity to accommodate one, and the saw must have enough power to make the cut, which can often be three to five times wider than a standard saw kerf. Dado blades are available in two types: **stack** and **adjustable**. Adjustable dado blades have the advantage of allowing you to fine-tune the cut to the exact thickness of the mating stock—a significant advantage when working with plywood. Dado blades can be intimidating because they create lots of dust, noise, and vibration.

On the other hand, using a router to cut these joints has several advantages, including smoother and more uniform joints and being able to move the tool across a large workpiece rather than moving the workpiece through the tool. The router's ability to work on stationary workpieces makes it particularly suitable for small shops, where moving larger pieces, such as plywood sheets through a tablesaw, is impractical. And although routers, like saws, also make a lot of dust, most offer much more effective dust collection when used in conjunction with a shop vacuum.

Because even large routers can struggle to cut sizable joints, it's best to make the joints in two or more passes for a cleaner result and to prevent overworking the router's motor. When stock isn't perfectly flat, as is often the case with plywood, a router may be the only way to achieve uniform joint depth. Its small base will ride on an uneven surface that would "tent" over a tablesaw blade.

When making any joint with a tablesaw or a router, do the initial setup on scrap pieces to check the fit. The scales on saws and routers may not be as precise as the work requires, so first set the blade height or bit depth with a measuring rule, and then confirm the dimensions with test cuts. In the end, you'll always need to cut to fit.

To make uniform cuts on a tablesaw, the stock must be as flat as the saw's table, or else it will ride over the saw blade and prevent it from cutting to the desired depth. If the stock isn't flat, using a router is the better choice. But before you do any cutting, consider executing a "fly-through" to understand the dynamics of making the cut. With the saw's blade lowered below the table surface, or the router's bit retracted or removed, go through the physical motion of moving the stock across the saw table or the router across the stock. This will give you an idea of how to position your body and the physical effort required to complete the cut. It's important to execute the cut in one smooth motion because stopping mid-cut can cause a choppy, uneven cut—or worse, burning and kickback.

Dust-collection port

Routers can create a lot of dust and have a way of kicking it everywhere. A dust-collection port built into the base and a good vacuum will allow you to keep the debris under control.

Using Glues & Fasteners

Choosing the appropriate glue and fasteners is actually fairly straightforward for most basic small-shop projects. Yellow glue is the most sensible choice for many woodworking projects, because it's easy to apply, has a long open time, and creates a very strong bond when used properly. Cyanoacrylate (super glue) and polyurethane are also acceptable for many types of projects when a fast set time and water resistance are needed.

For woodworking glue to provide any strength, there must be at least two long-grain mating surfaces of the joint. That's because glue does not adhere well to end grain (cut across the grain), so a joint that depends on bonded end grain has no strength and is susceptible to failure. However, when working with solid wood, there's often no need for mechanical fasteners at all when more complex joints, such as mortise-and-tenon joints, are used. That's because these joints are made by mating long-grain surfaces.

On the other hand, it's almost always necessary to use some sort of mechanical fastener with plywood and solid wood projects that are put together with butt joints because of exposed end grain. Dowels and biscuits are the most "refined" mechanical fasteners for these types of projects because they're totally hidden and create glued long-grain surfaces that are inherently strong. However, they do require special equipment—a doweling jig or a biscuit joiner—and somewhat more skill to pull off than using other types of fasteners.

Nails are the easiest fasteners to use, particularly with a nail gun, but they don't create joints with much strength. It's not easy to keep joints from slipping apart while nailing them, and nails don't have much holding power. Nailed projects depend on cumulative strength of the entire structure to hold together; the individual joints aren't that strong.

Screws are always a good compromise; they're easier to use than biscuits or dowels and stronger than nails, and there are screws for every application. All you need is a drill and a few bits, although a pocket-hole jig can locate screws in less obvious spots and help move the work along at a faster pace. Even exposed countersunk screw heads can be hidden with wood plugs to improve the appearance.

If portability is a requirement, knock-down fasteners are the way to go. Cross-dowels, threaded inserts, joint connectors, and hanger bolts are just a few of the available knock-down fittings. They're inexpensive, exceptionally strong, and fairly easy to install—a drill, a screwdriver, and a wrench are the only tools you'll need.

When gluing large surfaces, it's a good practice to spread the glue evenly for the best possible bond. Yellow wood glue should be applied to both sides of the joint.

Pocket-hole screws are driven at an angle using a specialized jig through the mating workpieces from either the inside or the outside.

Threaded inserts are one of many types of mechanical knock-down fasteners that are useful for shop applications, such as jigs and fixtures. The fastener is driven in from the back and a bolt or knob (in this instance) can be used to attach the mating piece.

Measuring & Marking

The adage "measure twice, cut once" may seem obvious, but it's sage advice that's too often ignored at the expensive of time, money, and needless frustration. Measuring has its own valuable rules and tips that can save you from errors and aggravation.

When working on a project, always use the same tape and rules and check them against each other to be sure they agree. Tape measures in particular are notorious for varying from one example to the next. The end hooks are usually the source of the deviation. Tapes are fine for measuring basic stock cutoffs, but use a high-quality steel rule for precise work.

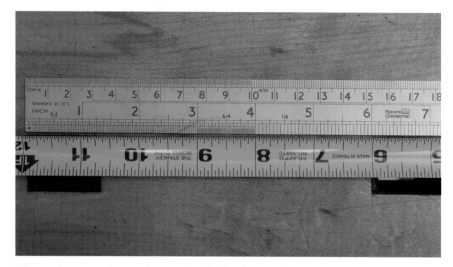

When using more than one measuring device for a project, always check that they read the same. Surprisingly, there are some rules and tapes that don't provide the same measurements.

Using a story stick is a good way to avoid making a measuring mistake. Once you have a set of measurements for a project, mark them on a stick and then use the stick rather than a tape or rule to mark workpieces.

When repeatedly using the same measurements for a project, make a "story stick." It's simply a wooden stick marked with your project's most-used measurements. It can save you from mistakes caused by misreading a tape or rule. A combination square can also act as a type of story stick—it's great for following an edge to mark a continuous line. Even with careful measuring, there's no substitute for checking the fit of each joint as you make it.

What you use to mark measurements and layout depends on the tolerances of the project. A carpenter's pencil is fine for rough work, but a fine mechanical pencil or sharp knife is more appropriate for furniture making. Scoring on a cutline with a knife also prevents splintering when you cut the piece.

Marking a layout on workpieces isn't required, but it helps keep your workflow organized and prevents mistakes. Label pieces with painter's tape with information such as what's left and right, front and back, and inside and outside. You can put a lot of information on a piece of tape and it won't mar your workpiece.

As the number of parts for a project increases, so does the potential for getting them mixed up. By marking parts with tape labels that have clear directions, the chances of making an error are greatly reduced.

Smoothing Surfaces

The surface of most wood from home centers and lumberyards will have coarse sanding marks or fine ripples from milling that will detract from a project's finished appearance. Sanding is the most common method of removing these blemishes and also for leveling joints and refining the surface after a project is assembled. It often makes sense to do most sanding before assembling a project. Sanding parts before they're assembled saves time, so once they're assembled it's just a matter of leveling joints and doing some final touchup. There are times when a hand plane or scraper might be faster and do a better job, but sanding is quick and doesn't require as much skill as using the hand tools.

Final sanding is best done by hand, because orbital pad sanders can leave swirl marks on the wood. Use a sanding block when hand sanding to maintain a flat, even worksurface and to help prevent hand fatigue. There are several other types of abrasive products that are useful in a small shop, such as sanding sponges and steel wool. They're practical for jobs such as wet-sanding, removing rust, and buffing metal.

The size of the sandpaper's abrasive coating is indicated by a number; lower numbers are coarser

SANDPAPER GRIT	USE
60- to 80-grit	Coarse sanding, such as removing old finishes
100- to 120-grit	Removing wood stock quickly
180-grit	Removing sanding scratches in wood
220- to 320-grit	Smoothing to a final finish

Sometimes a hand plane is good substitute for sanding. A plane can produce a glass-smooth surface. Keeping a plane tuned can be daunting at first but the results can be worth the effort.

and higher numbers are finer. Having about four grades on hand will allow you to handle most tasks.

Although there are several kinds of sandpaper, there are two types that will meet most needs in a small shop, because they can be used with wood, metal, and plastic. **Aluminum oxide** sandpaper is the most common type of general-purpose paper that can be used with power sanders or for hand sanding. **Silicon carbide** has similar characteristics and is more aggressive than aluminum oxide, but it does wear out faster. Some types of silicon carbide with water-resistant backings are also used for wet/dry sanding.

You'll also find sandpaper labeled "open coat" and "closed coat." The former is less prone to clogging and is best for power sanding, while the latter sands more aggressively and is better for hand sanding. Another type that's resistant to clogging is called stearated paper, which has a soapy coating that repels dust. Sanding products also come with cloth backing and film backing that are more flexible and are ideal for hand sanding curves and in tight spaces.

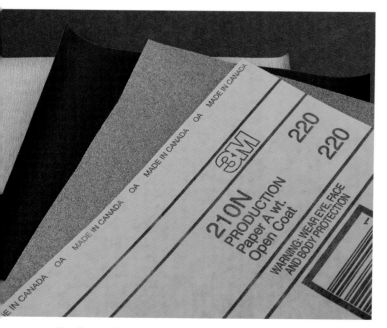

Sanding is the most popular way to smooth wood, so keep at least three grits on hand—medium to fine—and you'll be covered in most situations. Specialized papers such as stearated and wet/dry can come in handy too.

Assembling, Gluing & Clamping

Assembling a project is a bit like dancing—a matter of coordination and timing. All the parts, equipment, and supplies must be in the right place, and you need to know where they are so you can work quickly and complete the assembly before the glue sets. If a project is simple and has few parts, it can usually be assembled in one session. But complex projects may need to be assembled in stages or as sub-assemblies.

Determining the sequence of gluing parts should be done with a dry run. Here's a quick overview of a typical assembly:

- Have some cardboard or pads handy to protect the projecting from marring.

- Check to make sure that all of the project's parts fit together correctly by assembling them without glue.

- Determine how many and what types of clamps are needed. Adjust the clamp jaws close to the required opening distance so they can be quickly tightened and then stage them in convenient spots around the assembly area.

A simple trick when gluing parts together is to apply masking tape as close as possible to the edges being glued. Once the glue starts to set, pull off the tape to reveal a totally clean joint area.

- Gather all the other supplies that might be needed, including glue, a glue brush or spreader, rags, dowels or biscuits, a tape measure (to check for square), masking tape, a utility knife, a scraper or putty knife, clamp pads, a rubber mallet, and a few blocks of soft wood.

- Start applying glue to the joints. Spread the glue evenly—not too wet and not too dry—and on all mating surfaces (if using yellow glue). Work quickly so the glue doesn't have a chance to set.

- Begin clamping by placing all the clamps with light pressure, and then tighten them sequentially but don't over-tighten.

- In the case of a cabinet, check for square by measuring diagonally across the corners with a tape measure. Adjust if necessary.

- Glue squeeze-out is almost inevitable, but you can keep it from staining around joints by carefully applying masking tape to the adjoining edges of the joints before clamping. If that's not practical, wipe away the excess glue with a damp cloth or wait until it sets to a rubbery consistency and remove it with a sharp chisel.

- Leave the clamps on until the glue cures, which can be as long as 24 hours for yellow glue.

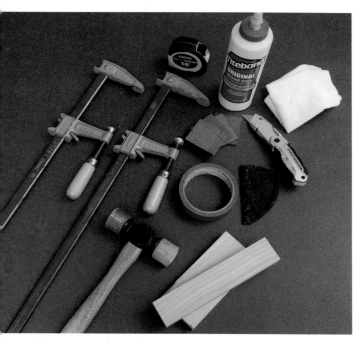

The best way to avoid panic when assembling a project is to stage all the items you typically use so you don't need to go looking for them.

Additional Techniques

As your woodworking skills improve, you'll look for more refined methods to achieve your goals. Here are a few helpful hints.

Cutting Curves

If you're cutting curves, you'll need a jigsaw or a bandsaw, or both. A jigsaw is better suited for cutting larger stock and plywood because of its portability. For small and narrow pieces, a bandsaw is the best choice. (It's also the best tool for resawing thick stock into thinner pieces.) But to cut smooth curves on a bandsaw, a narrow, fine-tooth blade is necessary. For example, with a bandsaw, a ¼-inch-wide blade with 10 teeth-per-inch (TPI) would be about right to cut curves in ¾-inch-thick wood, but with thinner material, more teeth are required. The blade's width will also determine how tight a curve it can cut. Use a push stick when cutting narrow pieces on a bandsaw.

The same basic principle applies to jigsaws, but the teeth are very different because of the tool's reciprocating action. When using a jigsaw, make sure the work is supported on both sides of the cut unless the cutoff portion is very narrow.

Mortise & Tenon Joints

Mortise-and-tenon joints provide excellent strength, but they have a somewhat intimidating reputation for being difficult to make. Although some forms of the joint are complicated to make, others are simple and can be achieved with basics tools. A dowel joint works on the same principle as a mortise-and-tenon joint, so if you use that concept as a starting point the rest is easy.

Here's an uncomplicated method to make mortise-and-tenon joints with floating tenons, which are essentially flat dowels.

- First you need to lay out the mortise in pencil or with a sharp knife. A rule of thumb for mortises is that they should be one-third as wide as the stock is thick.

- Next, you need to drill a series of closely spaced holes slightly smaller in diameter than the width

Mortise-and-tenon joints are at the more difficult end of the joint-making spectrum, but they do offer more strength and durability than most other common woodworking joints.

A simple way to make a mortise is to mark the joint, and then drill a series of holes inside the layout lines. The tape on the bit is to prevent drilling too deep.

After completing the holes, use a sharp chisel to clean out the waste and straighten the mortise wall. Floating tenons can be made by cutting strips to match the length and width of the mortises.

of the mortise to allow for any lateral movement when drilling the holes. For example, if the mortise is ¼ inch wide, use a ³⁄₁₆-inch-diameter bit. If possible, use a brad-point bit because it won't skate off-center on the stock like a standard twist bit might. The depth of the holes (tenon length) depends on the width of the stock, but for adequate strength they should be at least twice as deep as the mortise is wide. For good alignment, use a dowelling jig to drill the row of holes.

•   Once you've drilled the holes, clamp the workpiece in a vise and use a very sharp chisel to carefully pare away the waste between the holes.

•   Now cut matching mortises in the mating pieces.

•   Then cut pieces of stock to the same thickness as the mortise width to make the floating tenons. It's likely that you'll need to make adjustments to get a good fit, but this type of joint is every bit as strong as a conventional mortise-and-tenon joint.

Plate-joining biscuits are strong, provide near-perfect joint alignment, and are lightning fast to make. However, you'll need a biscuit joiner to cut the slots.

BENCHTOP PROJECTS

Bench-Top Clamp Cradles

It's often just the small things that make the difference between smooth sailing on a project and total frustration. That's where these bar- and pipe-clamp cradles come in. When gluing together boards to projects such as tabletops and door panels, it's most efficient to put the clamps on the bench top and then stack the boards to be glued between the clamp jaws. But most clamps aren't made to hold a "jaws up" position; they just roll over.

These cradles prevent the clamps from rolling over and keep the bars and pipes elevated off the bench. And the "feet" provide the clearance to slip extra clamps under the glue-up, if required. That allows you to focus exclusively on gluing and aligning the stock, so you won't need to struggle with maneuvering clamps into the right position.

Each clamp requires two cradles, and it's not unusual to use eight or more clamps for a glue-up. Note that you should alternate the clamps top and bottom when gluing a panel, so you'll only need enough cradles for the bottom clamps.

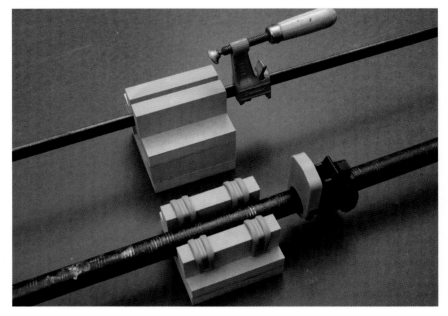

Clamp cradles are a "third hand" that keep glue-ups manageable. The height and opening of the cradles can be customized to accommodate any bar or pipe clamp.

Making the cradles is a simple task that requires a few hand tools and supplies. You'll also need a miter saw or a tablesaw to cut the parts.

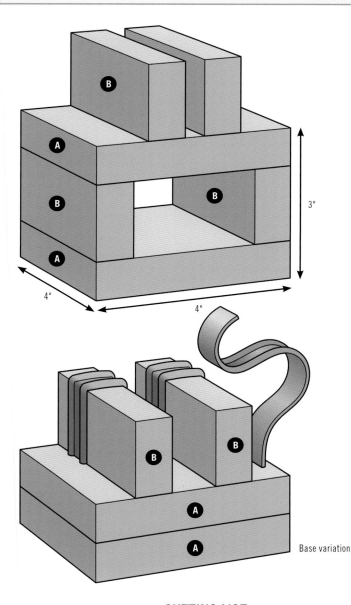

Base variation

TOOLS & MATERIALS

Eye & ear protection

Work gloves

Scraps of ¾" solid wood, plywood, or MDF

Miter saw or tablesaw

Combination square

Yellow wood glue

Hammer (or pneumatic nailer) or cordless drill

1½" finish nails

Self-adhesive rubber door or window insulation

Contact cement or cyanoacrylate (if needed)

CUTTING LIST

KEY	NO.	PART/MATERIAL	SIZE
A	2	Top/bottom, plywood	¾ × 4 × 4"
B	4	Feet/flanges, plywood	¾ × 1½ × 4"*

*Adjust the height of flanges to suit the bar or pipe size.

How to Make Bench-Top Clamp Cradles

Start by ripping lengths of 1½"-wide stock for the feet and flanges. (Note that you can modify the height of the flanges to suit the size of the clamp bar or pipe.) A miter saw (left) is the preferred tool to cut the parts. You can mark each cut or use a stop-block clamped to the right fence for repeatable cuts. If you use a tablesaw (right) to cut parts, the fence can be used for repeatable cuts, but you must clamp a block to the fence in front of the blade to prevent binding and kickback.

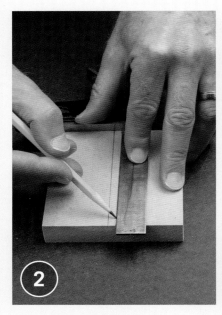

With a combination square, mark the positions of the clamp flanges. The distance between the flanges should be determined by the width of the bars or pipes. With bars, you can make the spacing very tight, just enough so they easily slip in and out. For pipe clamps, the spacing should be snug once the rubber strips are glued in. You'll probably need to experiment a little to get this right.

Test-fit the bar between the flanges for a snug fit. The height of the flanges can vary depending on how close the work needs to be to the clamp jaws.

Apply glue the top and the flange, and then press them together to spread the glue. Let the glue grab before continuing with nailing.

If you're nailing by hand, bore pilot holes for the nails. This is particularly important when using MDF or particleboard.

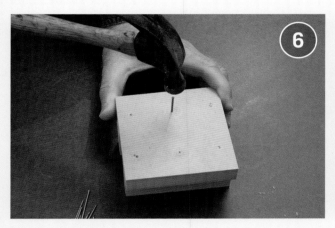

Once you've bored the pilot holes, use a tack hammer and 1½" finish nails to secure them.

Cut and glue on feet and a bottom, if necessary, to elevate the cradle so additional clamps can be slipped under the glue-up if needed. For some applications, you'll only need the flanges and the top.

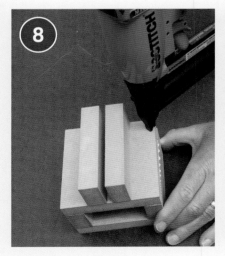

Nail the feed and bottom onto the flanges. An 18-gauge pneumatic brad nailer is an affordable tool that's convenient, is easy to use, and will greatly speed up assembly.

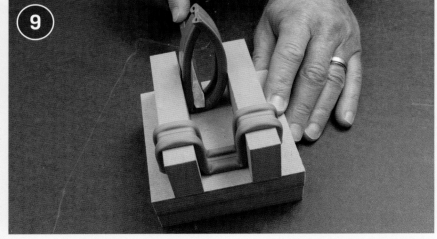

Pipe clamps can roll over, so apply self-adhesive rubber insulation to provide grip between the flanges. A screwdriver works well to press the material into place. If the rubber insulation isn't self-adhering, use some contact cement or cyanoacrylate to fasten the strips to the flanges on the pipe clamp cradles. Be sure to coat both sides of the work and let the contact cement dry before pressing them together.

Sandpaper & Blade Storage Box

Organization may be a never-ending process, but there are some classic storage projects that you should make for your shop right from the start. Because it's difficult to do any work without first having sandpaper and tablesaw/circular saw blades, creating storage for these workshop essentials should be on the top of your to-do list. And it's also logical for them to share a storage unit because they're of similar size and can be conveniently retrieved the same way—by pulling the shelves out for easy access. Or you can glue the shelves in place if you don't need them to slide. The finished box can sit on a shelf or bench, or be mounted on a wall with cleats.

You can make this storage box out of almost any ¾- or ½-inch plywood or hardboard scraps you have on hand. The plywood can be any grade depending on how you want the finished box to look. The minimum dimension of the shelves should be about 11 × 12 inches to accommodate standard 9 × 11-inch sandpaper sheets and 10-inch saw blades. Just increase the size of the parts if you need storage for 12-inch saw blades. This is one of the simplest projects you can make and requires only common shop tools.

A sandpaper storage box is also practical for keeping saw blades organized. Simple construction and sliding shelves make this a quick and versatile project.

SANDPAPER & BLADE STORAGE BOX

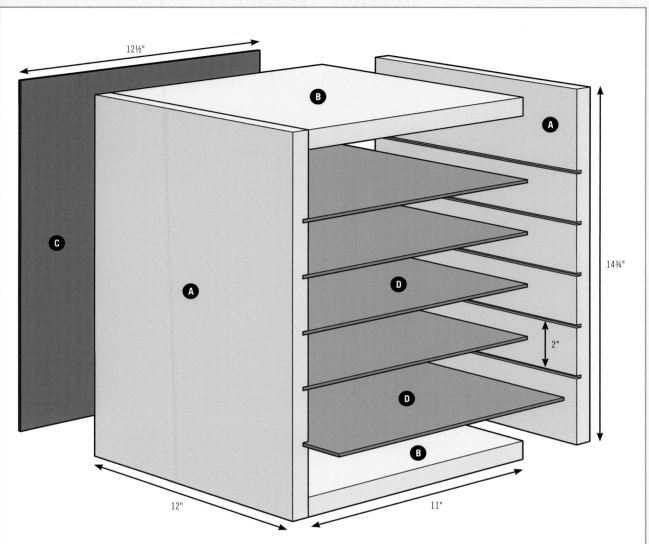

TOOLS & MATERIALS

Eye & ear protection

Work gloves

¾ × 24 × 48" plywood (1)

⅛ × 24 × 48" hardboard (1)

Tablesaw

Tape measure and pencil

Cordless drill with twist bits and a countersink bit

Yellow wood glue

Hammer or pneumatic brad nailer

½" and 1½" brad nails

No. 8 × 2" screws

Sandpaper

Clamps

CUTTING LIST

KEY	NO.	PART/MATERIAL	SIZE
A	2	Sides, plywood	¾ × 12 × 14¾"
B	2	Top/bottom, plywood	¾ × 11 × 12"
C	1	Back, hardboard	⅛ × 12½ × 14¾"
D	5	Shelves, hardboard	⅛ × 11½ × 12"

How to Make a Sandpaper & Blade Storage Box

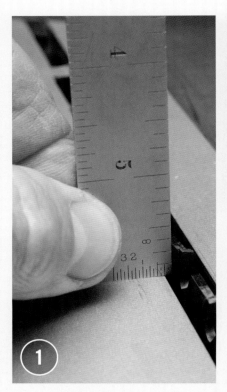

To cut the shelf dadoes, set the tablesaw blade slightly higher than ¼".

Begin by cutting the plywood and hardwood pieces with a tablesaw. Lay out the shelf dadoes (or grooves) on one of the sides and then transfer the marks to the other. This will help prevent cutting mistakes that can misalign shelves.

Make a few practice cuts on scrap to check the depth. With a standard ⅛" kerf blade, you'll need to make one or two passes for each shelf slot. When you run the sides through the saw, alternately cut the two pieces so the grooves are also identical, and check that the grooves are landing on the layout lines.

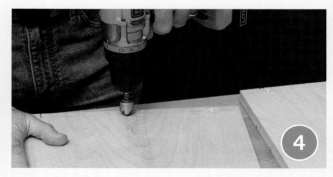

Strike a line ⅜" from the top and bottom edges of the sides for screw holes. Drill three evenly spaced clearance holes along the lines and then countersink the holes.

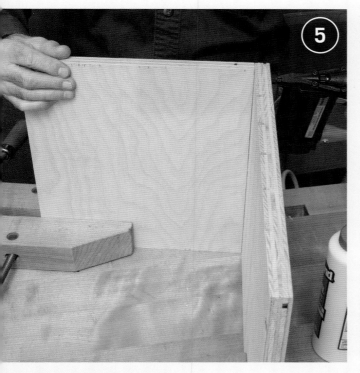

Apply wood glue to the edges, and then position a top/bottom and a side piece on the bench top so their mating edges meet at a right angle. Clamp the other edge of the top/bottom piece in a handscrew clamp or brace it against a solid backstop. Use a hammer or brad nailer to tack the pieces together.

Once the box is assembled, bore pilot holes into the top and bottom. This makes it easier to drive the screws and prevents them from splitting the plywood.

Now apply a small amount of glue to the mating surfaces and drive the screws. Repeat with the other two mating pieces and check that the grooves are matched. Assemble the box halves together with glue and screws. Adjust the drill's clutch to a setting that won't cause it to overdrive or strip the screw holes.

Now you can cut the back and shelves to fit. If the box is slightly out of square, you can use the back to force it into alignment. Fasten the back with glue and 1½" brads. Sand the shelf edges and then check that they fit and slide smoothly.

Push Sticks & Blocks

Keeping your fingers out of the path of spinning power-tool cutters is always a high priority in the shop. One of the best ways to do this is to use push sticks or blocks when moving narrow and irregular stock and small workpieces close to the blade. Because they're meant to take the beating that blades dish out, there's no point in making them too fancy. In fact, it makes sense to make several at a time so you'll always have an extra one on hand.

Push sticks come in handy especially with a tablesaw, bandsaw, and router table. Although there are countless styles of push sticks, they're mostly variations on the **stick type** or the **shoe type**. The stick type has a handle on one end and a V-notch on the other to hook the wood. It's best for pushing short and small workpieces and particularly useful when working on a bandsaw. The shoe type has a long front section to keep the stock pressed against the saw table and a lip (or heel) on the back to hook against the edge of the stock. It's the most versatile type and the least prone to slipping. Push blocks and pads

are meant for making non-through and edge-molding cuts and are a must if you use a jointer, as well as for some router table functions. Blocks have a lip to hook stock at the rear, with pads that have a rubber base and depend on downward pressure to control the stock. Basically, they're the same device with a slightly different base.

A push stick (top) is an essential shop aid that keeps your hands well away from blades and cutters. Push blocks (bottom) and push pads are typically used to guide narrow and smaller pieces through jointers and router tables.

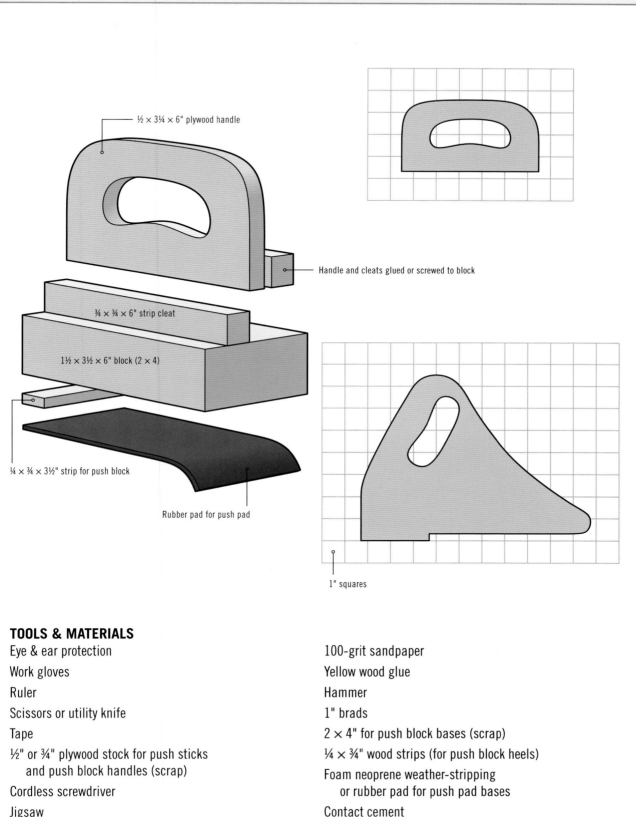

½ × 3¼ × 6" plywood handle

Handle and cleats glued or screwed to block

¾ × ¾ × 6" strip cleat

1½ × 3½ × 6" block (2 × 4)

¼ × ¾ × 3½" strip for push block

Rubber pad for push pad

1" squares

TOOLS & MATERIALS

Eye & ear protection

Work gloves

Ruler

Scissors or utility knife

Tape

½" or ¾" plywood stock for push sticks
  and push block handles (scrap)

Cordless screwdriver

Jigsaw

100-grit sandpaper

Yellow wood glue

Hammer

1" brads

2 × 4" for push block bases (scrap)

¼ × ¾" wood strips (for push block heels)

Foam neoprene weather-stripping
  or rubber pad for push pad bases

Contact cement

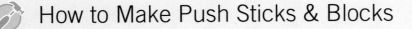

How to Make Push Sticks & Blocks

①

To make a push stick, start by drawing a 1" grid on a sheet of 8½ × 11" paper. This is used to scale up small drawings.

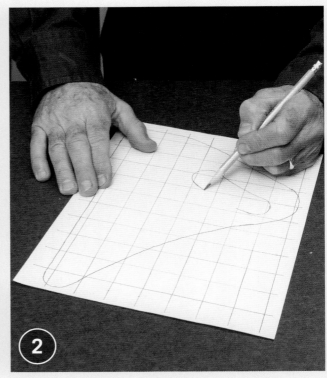

②

From a scaled-down pattern drawing, transfer the lines into the corresponding grid boxes. The transferred pattern doesn't need to be exact, just close.

③

Cut out the pattern with scissors or a utility knife and tape it to plywood stock; trace around the pattern with a pencil.

④

Another method is to heavily coat the back of the pattern with a carpenter's pencil to make "carbon paper."

Then, tape the coated paper to the plywood and retrace the pattern with sufficient pressure to transfer it to the plywood.

To prevent the plywood from splintering when it's cut, follow the pattern lines with a utility knife to cut the veneer.

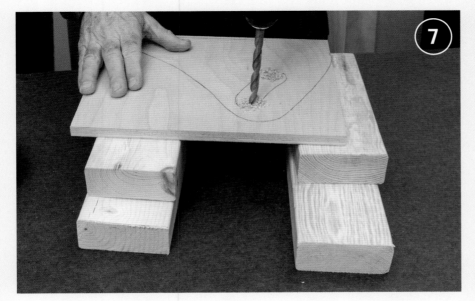

Before cutting the push stick's handhold, elevate the workpiece and bore starter holes that are large enough for the jigsaw blade to pass through.

(continued)

First, use a narrow, fine-tooth blade to cut the handhold, and then cut the outside of the pattern. Don't worry about being perfect; push sticks are disposable items.

You can use a small sander to smooth the edges and remove splinters. Pay special attention to the area around the handhold.

For a push block, cut out the handle just as you did with the push stick; start with the inside cut and then cut the outside.

After easing the handle's edges, glue and nail the cleats to the bottom of the handle. Align all the bottom edges carefully.

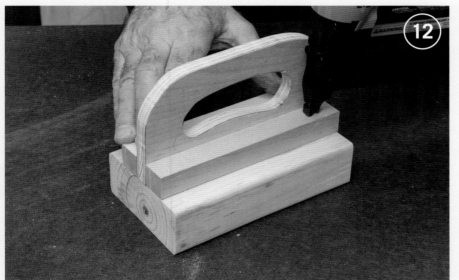

Glue and nail the handle assembly to the base. A scrap 2 × 4 makes a good base for keeping hands far away from cutters.

Glue a thin strip of wood to the bottom of the base for the "heel" that catches on stock. Push pads are made the same but have rubber glued to the bottom.

Wall-Mounted Pipe- & Bar-Clamp Storage Rack

There's a saying in woodworking that asserts that any woodworking project you do will require every clamp you own, plus one. Because clamps are an indispensable part of the craft, it's possible to collect them faster than scrap wood. And it's also too easy just to pile them up in a corner, so making a good storage system for them becomes increasingly important as your collection grows.

Clamps come in a wide variety of shapes and sizes for myriad purposes. That means there's no one-size-fits-all storage solution. For example, handscrews and C-clamps need storage that's configured differently than pipe- and bar-clamp storage. Because of their length, the latter can occupy a great deal of shop space, so it helps to make the storage as compact as possible. This wall-mounted storage rack for pipe and bar clamps is designed to minimize the amount of wall space it occupies.

This is one of the easiest and fastest projects you can build. The total cost of the project should be less than $20. If the dimensions of this project aren't quite right for your shop or your clamps, it's easy to modify. There's nothing special about the size; it's the utility of the project that matters. The width of the slots can and should be sized to fit your clamps. If your clamps are smaller or larger than the ones shown, you can adjust the width of the slots and the space between them for even more capacity.

The capacity and type of clamps this rack accommodates can be easily modified by making it wider and changing the width of its slots.

WALL-MOUNTED PIPE- & BAR-CLAMP STORAGE RACK

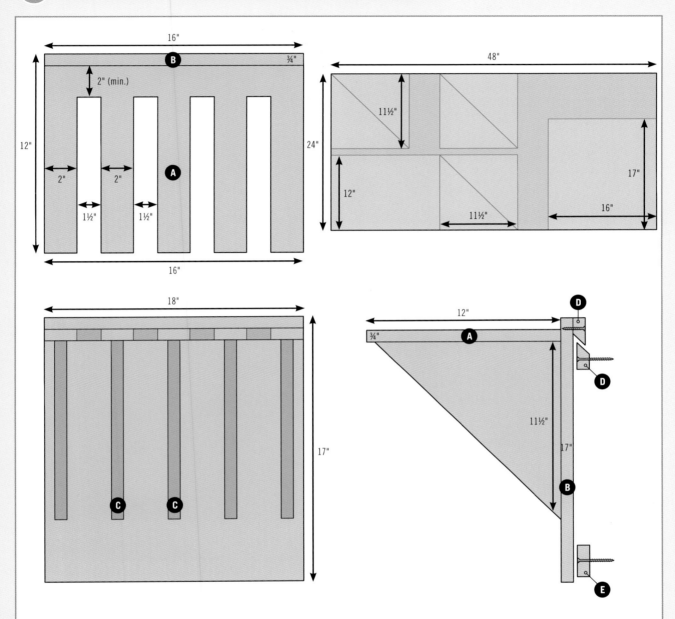

TOOLS & MATERIALS

Eye & ear protection

Work gloves

¾ × 24 × 48" plywood (1)

¾ × 4 × 48" solid wood
(poplar or pine)

Straightedge

Jigsaw

Utility knife

Combination square

C-clamps

100-grit sandpaper

Oscillating multi-tool
(optional)

Yellow wood glue

1½" brad nails

Brad nailer (optional)

No. 8 × 3" screws

Hollow-wall anchors (for
mounting on drywall)

Level

CUTTING LIST***

KEY	NO.	PART/MATERIAL	SIZE
A	1	Top shelf, plywood	¾ × 12 × 16"
B	1	Back, plywood	¾ × 16 × 17"
C	5	Gussets, plywood*	¾ × 11½ × 11½"
D	2	Cleat, solid wood**	¾ × 1½ × 17"
E	1	Balancing block, solid wood	¾ × 2 × 17"

*Triangles are cut diagonally from 11½ × 11½" squares.

**Both parts are cut from one 3"-wide piece.

***Suggested dimensions. Modify to fit your clamps
and available space.

How to Make a Wall-Mounted Pipe- & Bar-Clamp Storage Rack

Lay out the cuts on a sheet of 24 × 48" plywood (see cutting diagram). Almost any plywood will do, but use a higher grade for a more attractive result. Use a straightedge guide to guide the jigsaw's base to ensure straight cuts, score cutlines with a utility knife to prevent the veneer from shipping, and turn off the orbital action. Make sure the 90-degree corners of the gusset are square. Lay out the slots for the clamp on the top with a combination square. The top's 16" width is the right amount of space to house four slots.

Cut the slots with a jigsaw guided by a straightedge clamped to the top and the workbench. Use a fine-tooth blade for a smooth cut. The width of the slots in the top shelf should be wide enough to accommodate the clamp's pipes or bars, but not so wide that the clamp isn't supported by the shelf.

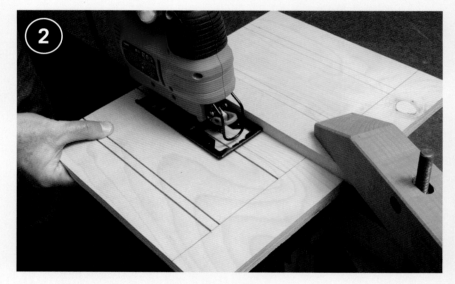

To finish cutting the slots, make cuts from each side into the opposite corner, and then square the corner by making light cuts to file out the waste. Use a narrow blade to negotiate the tight space at the back of the slots; for wider clamp slots, transition the back of the slots to a curve for strength.

Sand the inside and edges of the slots with 100-grit sandpaper. An oscillating multi-tool with a sanding attachment makes this job easy.

Cut the gussets from plywood squares. Try to stay on the cutlines, but it's not essential to make a perfect cut.

Check to make sure that the gusset triangles are square to ensure that the clamps will hang plumb when the completed rack is mounted. Sand the edges of the gussets smooth with a sander.

(continued)

Mark the position of all the screws that fasten the back to the top shelf and the gussets, and the top shelf to the gussets. Note that the screws are all driven into the top shelf "fingers," not the slots. Bore screw clearance holes and countersinks in the top and back. Back up the workpieces with scrap lumber to prevent splintering.

Start assembly by first applying glue and then shoot a few brad nails to position the parts before fastening them with screws.

Make sure the screw holes are located far enough down the gussets so they don't penetrate the opposite edge.

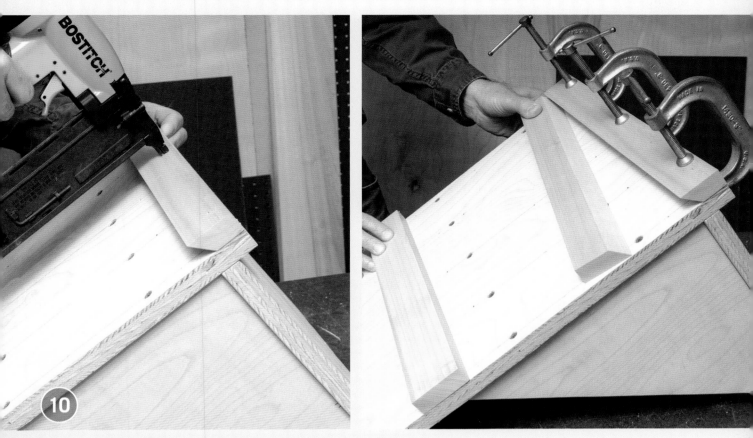

10

The rack can be mounted on the wall in several ways. The easiest is to mount it directly to wall studs, but we are using a French cleat, which we bevel-cut on a tablesaw. The cleat can be made by cutting a 3"-wide piece of solid wood in half at a 45-degree angle. Attach the top portion of the cleat to the rack, beveled angle facing down, with glue and screws or nails. If you use nails, clamp it as well. The balancing block is also attached to the wall to keep the rack plumb once it's mounted.

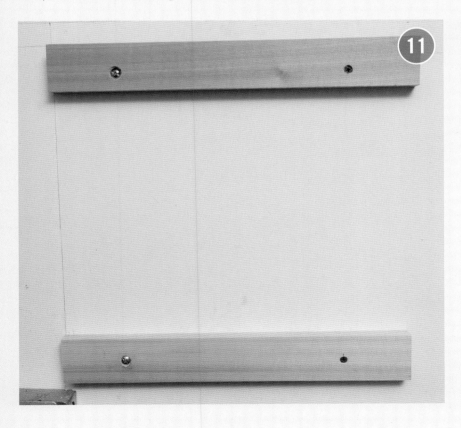

11

Mount the other half of the cleat and the balancing block to the wall with screws or hollow-wall anchors. Either way you mount the rack, use a level to strike a mounting line to ensure the clamps hang plumb. When using a French cleat, lock the rack to the wall by driving a few screws through the back into the balancing block.

Downdraft Sanding Box

The worst sort of dust in a shop is the extremely fine stuff that floats in the air and gets into everything, including your lungs. Power sanders are the worst offenders when it comes to making fine dust, but hand sanding isn't far behind. Most power sanders have a dust bag or a vacuum hook-up, but they're not always totally effective, particularly dust bags.

A downdraft box that's hooked up to a shop vacuum keeps the air and the dust around it moving in one direction—through the holes in the pegboard top into the vacuum. This box is relatively small and can be scaled up if you need to sand larger workpieces. Of course, the larger the box, the more suction you'll need. Most medium-size shop vacuums produce more than enough suction to work with this box. (If you have a dust extractor, you can adjust the suction so it's just the right amount.) It's important that your vacuum uses a high-quality filter and that its canister has a tight seal or it can blow dust back into the shop through the exhaust.

This project is a basic box and requires only beginner-level woodworking skills. Note that the top of the sanding box should not be glued down or fastened too tightly because it will wear and need to be replaced at some point.

A downdraft sanding box directs air through a pegboard top into a shop vacuum and keeps airborne dust from sanding under control.

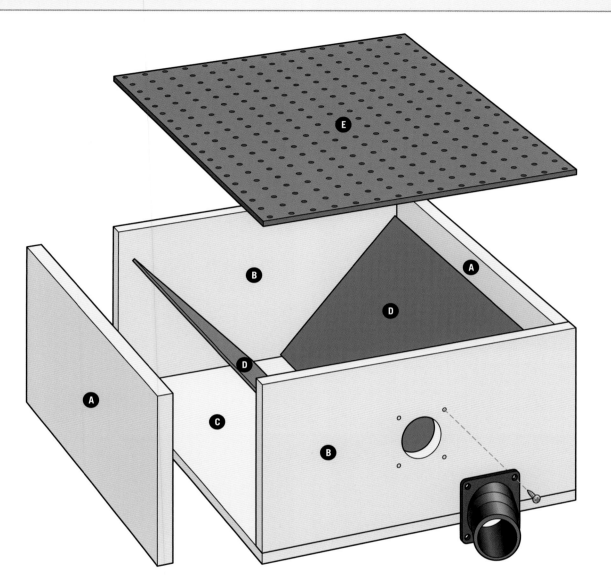

TOOLS & MATERIALS

Eye & ear protection

Work gloves

¾ × 24 × 48" plywood

⅛ × 24 × 24" hardboard

¼ × 24 × 24" pegboard

Tablesaw

Tape measure and pencil

Cordless drill with countersink bit

Jigsaw

Awl

Yellow wood glue and hot glue gun

Hammer or pneumatic brad nailer

1½" finish nails or pneumatic nails

No. 8 × 2" screws

½" plywood scrap (for bottom)

Rubber door bumpers
(optional, for base)

Combination square

Vacuum hose coupler

CUTTING LIST

KEY	NO.	PART/MATERIAL	SIZE
A	2	Sides, plywood	¾ × 8 × 18½"
B	2	Front/back, plywood	¾ × 8 × 16"
C	1	Bottom, plywood	½ × 16 × 20"
D	2	Baffles, hardboard	⅛ × 10 × 18½"
E	1	Top, pegboard	¼ × 16 × 20"

Cut the pieces from the plywood, hardboard, and pegboard using a tablesaw or jigsaw. Find the center of the front piece by drawing lines from opposite corners; where the lines of the "X" meet is the center of the board.

Using the vacuum connector as a pattern, trace around the outside of the connector to mark the hole in the front piece.

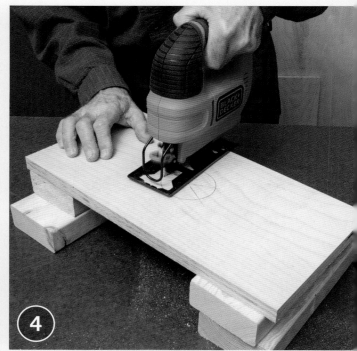

Bore a starter hole inside the circle, large enough to fit a narrow blade for your jigsaw.

With your jigsaw and a narrow fine-tooth blade, cut carefully inside the line. Prop the workpiece on scrap 2 × 4s to elevate it enough so the blade doesn't hit the bench. Check the fit of the connector; it should fit snugly. You'll glue or screw it to the front later.

Measure ⅜" from the edges of the front and back to mark screw hole centerpoints. Punch the centers with an awl as starter points for drilling.

Bore clearance holes that are slightly smaller than the screw shank and keep the drill as perpendicular to the work as possible.

Next, use a countersink bit to drill recesses for the screw heads. Avoid making them too deep or it can weaken the joint.

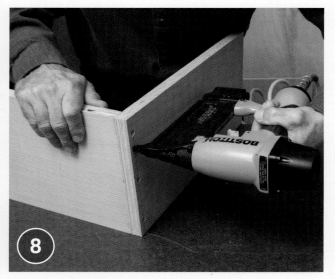

To make assembly easier and more precise, apply glue and then use a pneumatic brad nailer to hold the box together.
(continued)

Now bore pilot holes for screws into the adjoining sides. This will make it easier to drive the screws and help prevent splitting.

Drive the screws using the drill's slower speed and adjust the clutch to a setting that prevents the screws from being overdriven.

Fasten the bottom with glue and 1½" pneumatic or finish nails. Use the bottom to square the box if necessary. Make sure that the bottom's edges are flush with all the sides. To reduce vibration and to keep the box from sliding, you can apply rubber door bumpers to the bottom.

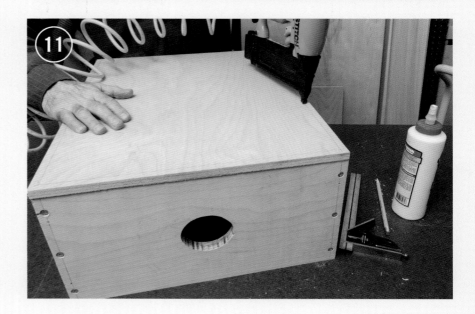

Attach the dust port to the front with screws. Dust ports like this are available from several online woodworking sources. You can also attach the port with polyurethane glue, which adheres to both wood and plastic.

Place the hardboard baffles in position and run a bead of hot glue along the edges with an electric glue gun. The baffles direct the airflow inside the box toward the vacuum. (If you don't have a glue gun, use yellow glue instead.)

Use a few screws to hold the pegboard top in place. Make sure the screws are sunk below the surface so they don't damage any workpieces. Although it's not elegant, you could even use duct tape to secure the top. The top gets a lot of wear, so make it easy to remove and replace.

Simple & Sturdy 2 × 4 Workbench

A workbench is the focal point of every shop, regardless of its size. But small shops need a bench that's flexible and in scale with its surroundings. This easy-to-build bench is made of common, inexpensive construction materials, but that doesn't detract from its sturdiness and durability. The simple butt-jointed design makes it convenient to modify any dimension or material to suit your requirements.

The MDF or particleboard top can be substituted with a butcher-block hardwood top if you want a material that's more suitable for heavy-duty tasks like furniture making. If your work tends to be hard on bench tops, consider covering the top with ⅛-inch hardboard that's tacked down in a few places so it can be easily replaced. If your floor isn't flat, you could add leg levelers or retractable casters for a mobile bench. As you gain experience, you can build on this basic design by adding drawers, enclosed storage, bench dogs, a bench vise, and other accessories.

This is a basic carpentry project that requires beginner skills and only a few tools, and it can be completed in four to eight hours. The materials are available at any home center or hardware store, and although the cost will vary, it should be well under $100. The return benefit is immediate, because you'll have a convenient surface for staging future projects.

A basic 2 × 4 workbench provides a solid and versatile focal point on which to build your shop. This one is a quick, easy, and economical project.

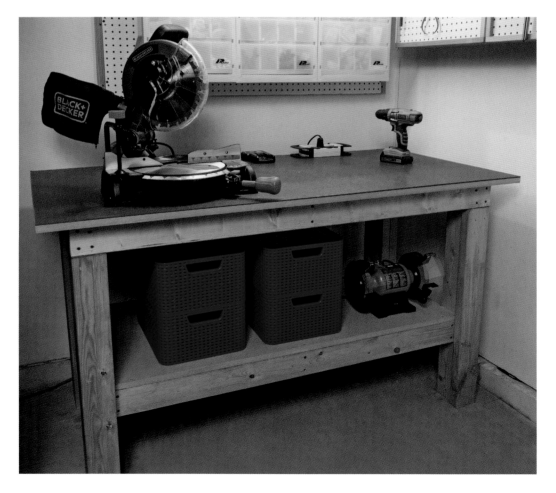

SIMPLE & STURDY 2 × 4 WORKBENCH

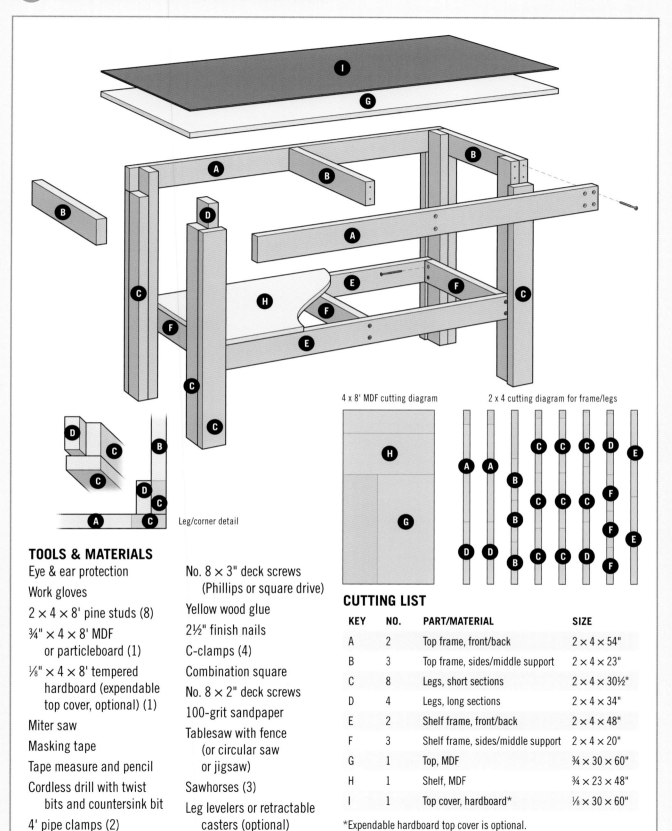

Leg/corner detail

4 x 8' MDF cutting diagram

2 x 4 cutting diagram for frame/legs

TOOLS & MATERIALS

Eye & ear protection

Work gloves

2 × 4 × 8' pine studs (8)

¾" × 4 × 8' MDF
  or particleboard (1)

⅛" × 4 × 8' tempered
  hardboard (expendable
  top cover, optional) (1)

Miter saw

Masking tape

Tape measure and pencil

Cordless drill with twist
  bits and countersink bit

4' pipe clamps (2)

No. 8 × 3" deck screws
  (Phillips or square drive)

Yellow wood glue

2½" finish nails

C-clamps (4)

Combination square

No. 8 × 2" deck screws

100-grit sandpaper

Tablesaw with fence
  (or circular saw
  or jigsaw)

Sawhorses (3)

Leg levelers or retractable
  casters (optional)

CUTTING LIST

KEY	NO.	PART/MATERIAL	SIZE
A	2	Top frame, front/back	2 × 4 × 54"
B	3	Top frame, sides/middle support	2 × 4 × 23"
C	8	Legs, short sections	2 × 4 × 30½"
D	4	Legs, long sections	2 × 4 × 34"
E	2	Shelf frame, front/back	2 × 4 × 48"
F	3	Shelf frame, sides/middle support	2 × 4 × 20"
G	1	Top, MDF	¾ × 30 × 60"
H	1	Shelf, MDF	¾ × 23 × 48"
I	1	Top cover, hardboard*	⅛ × 30 × 60"

*Expendable hardboard top cover is optional.

Cutting the MDF top with a circular saw requires a guide fence to ensure a straight cut. Here's how to do it.

Position the blade on the cutline and mark the edge of the saw's base.

Draw a line across the stock from the base edge mark, parallel with the cutline. Then clamp a straightedge on the line to guide the saw.

Make the cut, pressing the saw's base against the straightedge while making the cutting pass. It's best to make the cuts to the outside of the workpiece so a slip won't ruin it.

TIP

This bench should be built in sub-assemblies: the top frame, shelf frame, and legs. That results in a more controlled process and ensures the bench will be square and sit solidly on the floor. Start by cutting all the 2 × 4 pieces of the same dimensions, using the cutting chart to minimize waste. The chart shows how all the parts can be cut from eight 2 × 4s, and you risk needing more lumber if you ignore it. Label each 2 × 4 with the names of the parts to be cut to avoid confusion and mistakes. By themselves, the top and shelf frame aren't that strong, but once all the bench parts are joined together the structure will be very sturdy.

How to Make a Simple & Sturdy 2 × 4 Workbench

Beginning with the pieces for the top frame, cut all pieces to size. This will be easiest with a miter saw, which will ensure straight cuts. Use tape labels to mark the pieces corresponding to the part names in the diagram. This will simplify construction.

Mark the centerline positions for the sides and middle on the front and back pieces, and then on the inside center of the front and back frame parts for the middle support. Then mark for two screw holes in each joint, about ¾" from the edges of the stock.

Bore ⅛" pilot holes for 3" deck screws through the front and back into the sides and middle support and countersink for the screw heads. Deck screws are preferred because their threads extend the entire length of the screw, and they're relatively inexpensive.

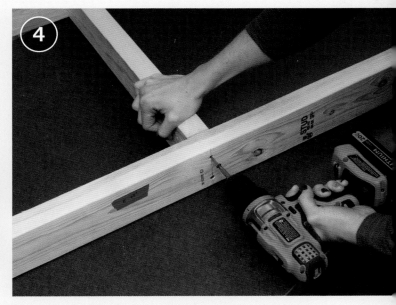

Place the middle and sides between the front and back. Use pipe clamps to gently hold the parts together. Make sure the parts are flush on all the edges before driving screws. Start with the middle support, and then fasten the ends. Now repeat the process to build the shelf frame. It's important that both frames are square, so measure diagonally from corner to corner. The measurements should be identical, and if they're not, torque the frame corners slightly to square them. The frames don't need to be totally perfect now; you'll be able to fix any deviation when you add the top and shelf. *(continued)*

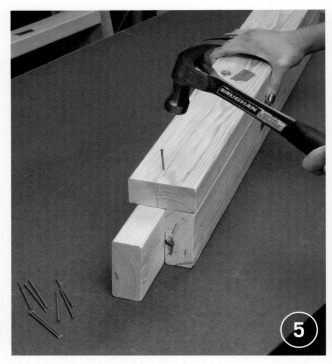

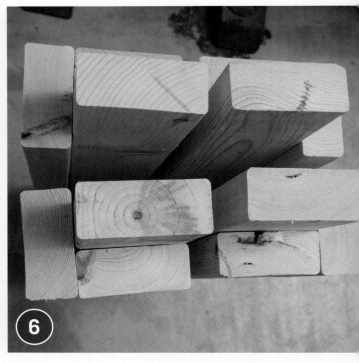

Now build the legs, using three 2 × 4s for each. First, cut all pieces to length using a miter saw. Glue and nail the three pieces for each leg using 2½" finish nails. When doing this, make sure the bottom ends are all flush with each other by bracing them against a solid surface, such as a wall or the floor. Spreading the glue evenly on all mating surface will help increase the strength of the bond.

Note that the leg pairs are mirror images of one another—left, right, front, and back. You'll need to get this right or you'll wind up with scrap lumber.

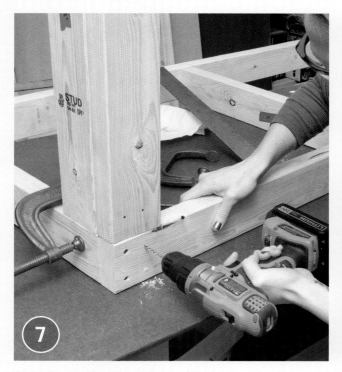

Apply glue to all mating surfaces of the legs and top frame, and then clamp the leg in place with a C-clamp. Check for square and then bore pilot holes for the screws. Attach the legs with 3" deck screws.

Mark the bottom edge of the shelf frame position on the legs with a combination square. Note how the leg is also screwed to the top frame from the inside.

Apply glue to the shelf frame and legs, and then clamp the legs to the frame. Check to make sure that the assembly is square and drive the screws.

Now cut the workbench top and shelf from a single sheet of 4 × 8' MDF or particleboard. Be sure to use a fine-tooth blade for the smoothest cut possible. Install the bottom shelf with 2" countersunk screws; glue is optional. If the shelf frame is out of square, nudge it flush with the edges of the shelf.

Now install the workbench top. You can install the top by driving screws through the top into the frame. For a cleaner look, you can drive screws from underneath diagonally through the frame or add cleats for screws to the inside of the frame. You just need to be careful not to penetrate the top with the tips of the screws. Note that the top has 3" of overhang on the sides and 2" on the front and back.

Finally, ease any sharp or rough edges with 100-grit sandpaper and the bench will be ready for your next project.

Shop Step Stool

A small stool that you can tuck under your workbench, store in a corner, or even hang on a wall is a great workshop project. Aside from providing more reach to high places, a small stool also offers a visual and leverage advantage when making parts on your bench and when assembling larger projects. This stool's width provides secure footing, and it has a roomy drawer mounted under the bottom step to store shop essentials, such as a utility knife, screwdrivers, a tape measure, and masking tape. The stool's small size makes it easy to store but still provides the extra reach you'll need for most situations.

Although it's not essential, the stool will be more attractive and sturdier if you use cabinet-grade plywood, such a birch, maple, or baltic birch. This type of plywood typically has more core plies, which makes it more rigid. You can use pine, oak, maple, or almost any other wood for the solid parts.

This project is simple but does require a fair degree of precision to make. The stool should take a day or less to build and cost about $60.

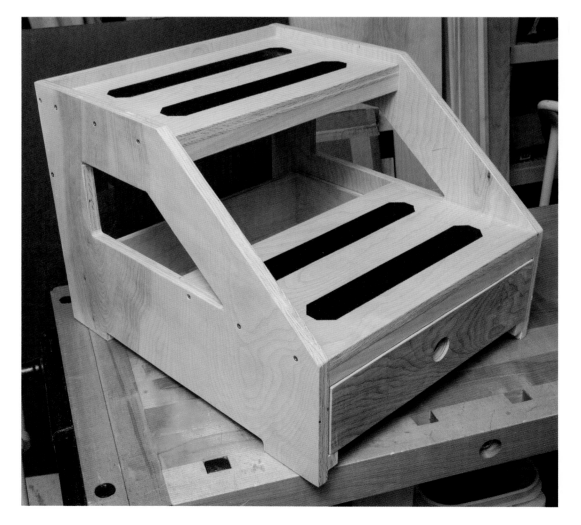

A step stool is essential in any shop. This one is lightweight, extremely stable, and sturdy, and has a handy drawer for tools and shop supplies.

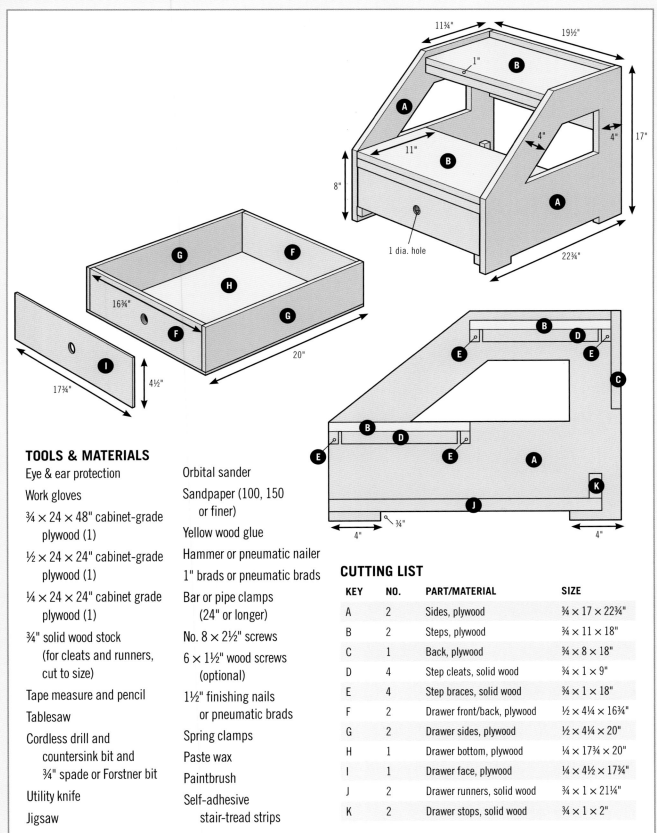

SHOP STEP STOOL

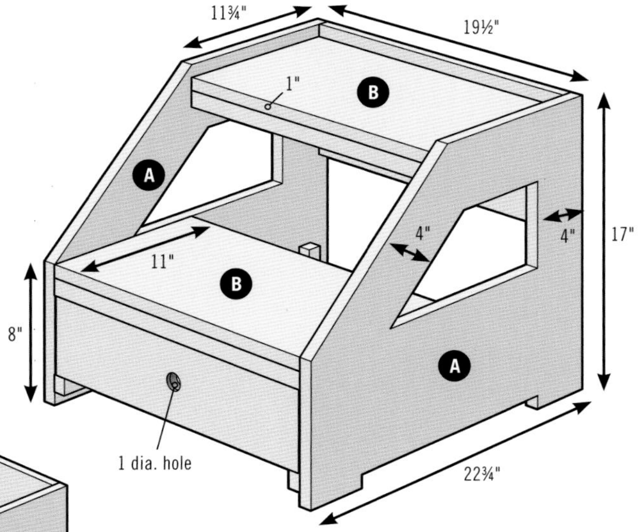
11¾"
19½"
1"
B
A
4"
4"
17"
11"
B
8"
A
1 dia. hole
22¾"

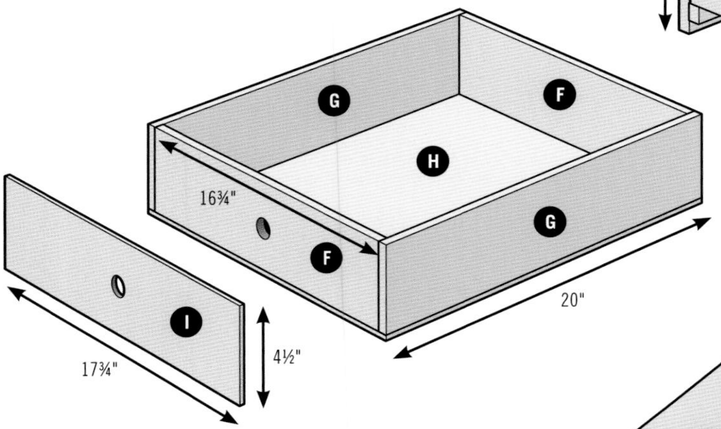
G
F
H
16¾"
G
F
I
20"
4½"
17¾"

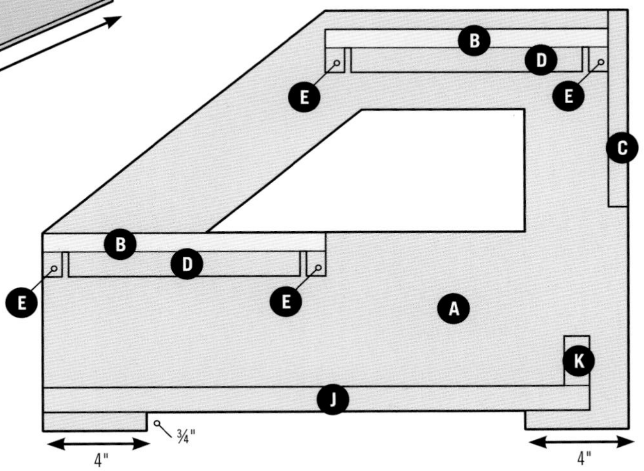
B
D
E
E
C
B
D
E
E
A
K
J
¾"
4"
4"

TOOLS & MATERIALS

- Eye & ear protection
- Work gloves
- ¾ × 24 × 48" cabinet-grade plywood (1)
- ½ × 24 × 24" cabinet-grade plywood (1)
- ¼ × 24 × 24" cabinet grade plywood (1)
- ¾" solid wood stock (for cleats and runners, cut to size)
- Tape measure and pencil
- Tablesaw
- Cordless drill and countersink bit and ¾" spade or Forstner bit
- Utility knife
- Jigsaw
- Orbital sander
- Sandpaper (100, 150 or finer)
- Yellow wood glue
- Hammer or pneumatic nailer
- 1" brads or pneumatic brads
- Bar or pipe clamps (24" or longer)
- No. 8 × 2½" screws
- 6 × 1½" wood screws (optional)
- 1½" finishing nails or pneumatic brads
- Spring clamps
- Paste wax
- Paintbrush
- Self-adhesive stair-tread strips

CUTTING LIST

KEY	NO.	PART/MATERIAL	SIZE
A	2	Sides, plywood	¾ × 17 × 22¾"
B	2	Steps, plywood	¾ × 11 × 18"
C	1	Back, plywood	¾ × 8 × 18"
D	4	Step cleats, solid wood	¾ × 1 × 9"
E	4	Step braces, solid wood	¾ × 1 × 18"
F	2	Drawer front/back, plywood	½ × 4¼ × 16¾"
G	2	Drawer sides, plywood	½ × 4¼ × 20"
H	1	Drawer bottom, plywood	¼ × 17¾ × 20"
I	1	Drawer face, plywood	¼ × 4½ × 17¾"
J	2	Drawer runners, solid wood	¾ × 1 × 21¼"
K	2	Drawer stops, solid wood	¾ × 1 × 2"

How to Make a Shop Step Stool

Lay out the pieces to the outside, square dimension of the parts on the plywood stock using pencil. Arrange the parts so the grain orientation is the same for like pieces. Cut out all the parts on a tablesaw or with a jigsaw.

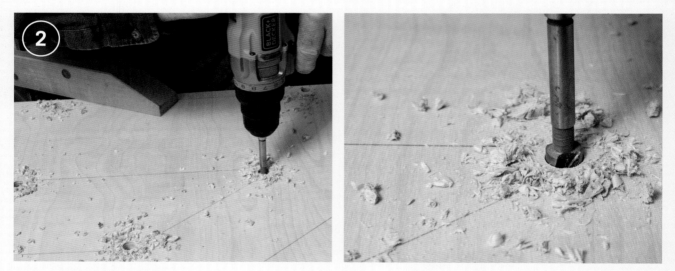

With a ½" Forstner bit, bore holes in all the corners of the handhold and bottom cutout. These will serve as entry points for the jigsaw blade and provide rounded corners.

Veneered plywood has a tendency to chip out when it's cross-cut, so scoring the cutlines with a utility knife can minimize this problem.

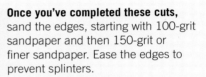

Now you'll need to cut the angle and cutouts on the side pieces. First use a jigsaw and a fence to cut the front angle. Turn off the orbital action of your jigsaw (if it has one) and use a fine-tooth blade to ensure a smooth cut. You may need to clamp or tack the fence to the workpiece. Now make the inside cutouts on the sides, using the pilot holes as access points for the saw blade. Finally, cut the foot slots on the bottoms of the side pieces. These help keep the stool from rocking when it's on a bumpy surface.

Once you've completed these cuts, sand the edges, starting with 100-grit sandpaper and then 150-grit or finer sandpaper. Ease the edges to prevent splinters.

Lay out the position of the bottom step cleats, drawer runners, and drawer stops on the sides. Be sure to leave 1" on each end of the step cleat for the step braces. Use glue and a pneumatic nailer to attach the cleats to the sides.

(continued)

Repeat the process to attach the top step cleats, again using glue and the pneumatic nailer. Locate and mark the centerline of the steps on the outside of both sides. Then mark the position for three screws on each centerline. Bore countersunk pilot holes for the screws.

Next, bore the three countersunk pilot holes in the sides for the back. Start assembly with the back and top step. If you have bar or pipe clamps, use them to gently hold the steps, back, and sides together as you fasten the top step and back to the sides with glue and No. 8 × 2½" screws. Drive a few screws through the back into the top step. Reinforce the joints by driving 1½" brads.

Check the width and depth of the drawer opening below the bottom step. The drawer should fit with a ¹⁄₁₆" to ⅛" gap between each side of the drawer front and the stool sides. You may need to tweak the dimensions of the parts slightly to achieve this fit. Cut all the drawer parts, then assemble the front/back and sides together first with 1" brads and glue.

Use the drawer bottom to square the drawer, then glue and nail it to the front, back, and sides.

Glue the drawer face to the drawer front and clamp lightly with spring clamps. Once the glue sets, bore a finger-hole drawer pull through the front with a ¾" spade or Forstner bit. Now check to make sure that the drawer slides smoothly. If it's a little rough, polish the drawer runner and the bottom edge of the drawer with paste wax.

A finish isn't required, but a water-based polyurethane or semigloss enamel paint is a good choice. Finally, apply some self-adhesive stair-tread strips to the steps to enhance traction.

Foldaway Wall Bench

Sometimes a workbench need be no more than a flat worksurface. If your work doesn't require accessories such a built-in vise, bench dogs, or additional storage, then a folding bench fits the bill.

This foldaway bench meets all those requirements, and it's also relatively inexpensive and easy to build. The bench has the added benefit of being wall mounted, so it folds flat and out of the way when not in use. If your shop is in a tight garage, it's an ideal platform for doing occasional tasks, such as working on lawn and garden equipment, servicing bicycles, and potting plants. But the bench can also be used inside the house as a crafts workstation for sewing, stained glass projects, jewelry making, scrapbooking, and many other hobbies.

This project requires only basic woodworking skills and should cost about $70 depending on the materials you purchase. It takes eight to twelve hours to build this bench, including painting and installation. All the materials can be purchased at almost any home center or hardware store. Precut two-by-four-foot plywood sheets are easy to transport and require less cutting in the shop, but some home centers and lumberyards will cut four-by-eight-foot sheets to size. Use birch plywood for the top and top supports—it provides a smooth, flat surface and void-free core. Particleboard or medium-density fiberboard (MDF) would also work and cost less, but it's heavier and won't wear as well. If you opt for pine rather than poplar, you can cut it to size from construction-grade lumber, such as two-by-fours, or use an interior-grade pine trim lumber.

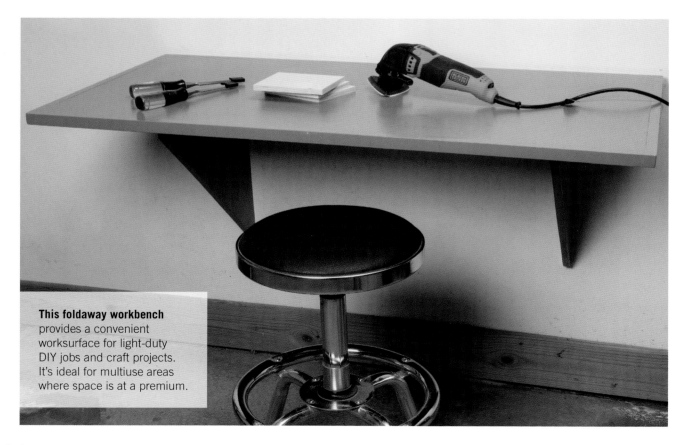

This foldaway workbench provides a convenient worksurface for light-duty DIY jobs and craft projects. It's ideal for multiuse areas where space is at a premium.

FOLDAWAY WALL BENCH

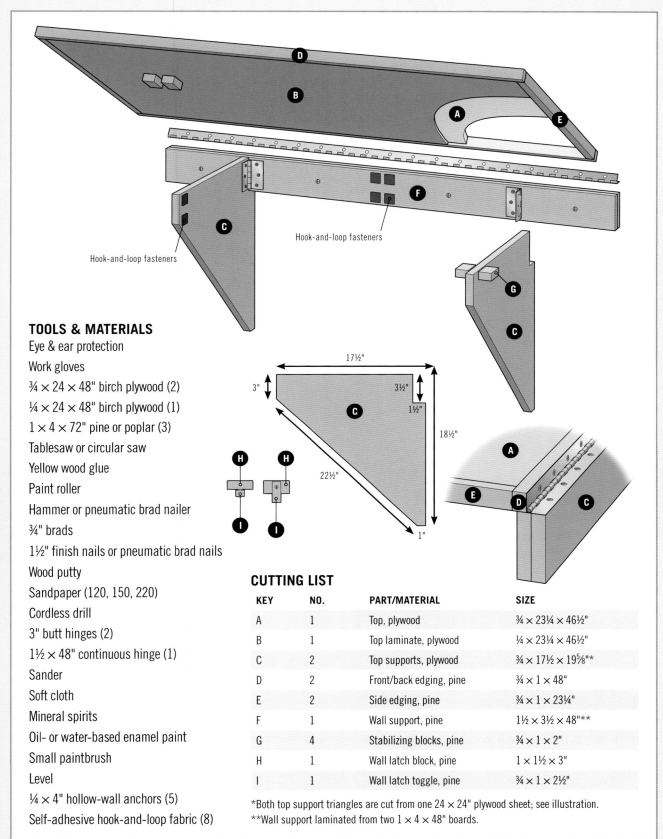

Hook-and-loop fasteners

Hook-and-loop fasteners

17½"

3"

3½"

1½"

18½"

22½"

1"

TOOLS & MATERIALS

Eye & ear protection

Work gloves

¾ × 24 × 48" birch plywood (2)

¼ × 24 × 48" birch plywood (1)

1 × 4 × 72" pine or poplar (3)

Tablesaw or circular saw

Yellow wood glue

Paint roller

Hammer or pneumatic brad nailer

¾" brads

1½" finish nails or pneumatic brad nails

Wood putty

Sandpaper (120, 150, 220)

Cordless drill

3" butt hinges (2)

1½ × 48" continuous hinge (1)

Sander

Soft cloth

Mineral spirits

Oil- or water-based enamel paint

Small paintbrush

Level

¼ × 4" hollow-wall anchors (5)

Self-adhesive hook-and-loop fabric (8)

CUTTING LIST

KEY	NO.	PART/MATERIAL	SIZE
A	1	Top, plywood	¾ × 23¼ × 46½"
B	1	Top laminate, plywood	¼ × 23¼ × 46½"
C	2	Top supports, plywood	¾ × 17½ × 19⅝"*
D	2	Front/back edging, pine	¾ × 1 × 48"
E	2	Side edging, pine	¾ × 1 × 23¼"
F	1	Wall support, pine	1½ × 3½ × 48"**
G	4	Stabilizing blocks, pine	¾ × 1 × 2"
H	1	Wall latch block, pine	1 × 1½ × 3"
I	1	Wall latch toggle, pine	¾ × 1 × 2½"

*Both top support triangles are cut from one 24 × 24" plywood sheet; see illustration.

**Wall support laminated from two 1 × 4 × 48" boards.

How to Make a Foldaway Wall Bench

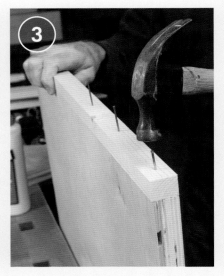

Cut all wood pieces to size, using a tablesaw or circular saw. To build the laminated top, apply yellow wood glue with a short-nap roller to both top surfaces. You'll need to work quickly because wood glue has a limited open time. (If your work doesn't need a bench top as robust as this, you can skip the lamination step—and save a little money.)

Align the edges of the plywood, and then use a pneumatic nailer or ¾" brads to secure the underlying ¼" sheet to the top ¾" sheet. The ¼" sheet is on the bottom side of the top, so the fasteners won't be visible when the bench is in use.

Fasten the edging to the laminated top. Start by fastening the side edging to the top with glue and 1½" finish nails or pneumatic brad nails, and then attach the front and back edging. The poplar or pine edging provides not only a more durable edge and a finished look but also a better grip for the continuous-hinge screws than a raw plywood edge would. Fill any holes or voids with wood putty, and then sand all the pieces and ease sharp edges as needed with 120-grit sandpaper.

Top support

Butt hinge

Stabilizing block

Wall support

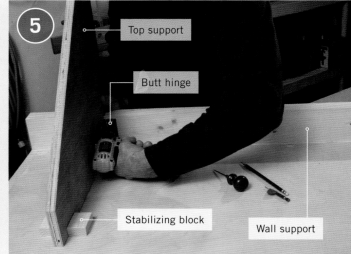

Cut the triangular top supports with a jigsaw. To prevent any interference, allow an extra ¹⁄₁₆" for the notches that wrap around the wall support. Next, glue two 1 × 4s together to make the wall support, or use a clear, straight 2 × 4. Lay out and cut the plywood top supports with a fence-guided jigsaw. Bore ¼" holes for the hollow-wall anchors in the wall support and in the latch parts. (Screws can be used instead of hollow-wall anchors where the support crosses wall studs.)

Fit the butt hinges precisely on the inside corner of the triangular supports to ensure that the top will be level. The hinge barrel must be centered between the two joined parts. Don't install all the screws until the fit is perfect.

6 Orient the continuous hinge so the knuckle is centered between the top and the wall support and there's enough clearance so the top can pivot without hitting the wall when mounted. Now you can paint the wall bench, if you so desire. Before painting, do a final sanding with 120- or 150-grit paper, and then wipe off any dust with a soft cloth moistened with a bit of mineral spirits. Apply the paint with a roller and small brush, allowing 24 hours between coats. Scuff-sand with 220-grit or finer sandpaper between coats to achieve a smoother final finish.

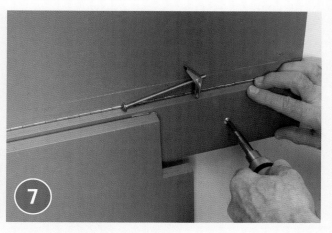

7 Level the assembled wall bench and mark its position on the wall. Mark the hole locations for the hollow-wall anchors or toggle bolts to secure the wall bench. If you're lucky enough for the bench to span a couple of 2 × 4 wall studs, use screws to mount the bench to the wall. Drill holes and install the hollow-wall anchors, and secure the bench.

8 Cut the stabilizing blocks that cradle the supports to hold them in position when the top is in use, and the wall latch parts that secure the top when it's in the stored position. Lift the bench top up flush against the wall, then mark the position of the wall latches on the wall. Bore holes in the drywall for the wall anchors and then install the anchors in the wall support before attaching the latches.

9 Attach pairs of stabilizing blocks to the bottom of the bench to hold the triangular supports in place when the bench is in the down position.

10 Attach hook-and-loop fastener pads (left) to the tips of the triangular supports and to the wall support to hold the supports against the wall when the bench is not in use. The photo above shows the proper orientation of the fastener pads and stabilizer blocks.

Folding Miter Saw Stand

Power miter saws were once regarded as a job-site-only tool that had just enough accuracy for framing cuts. But over the years the precision of miter saws improved, as did the quality of the blades. Woodworkers discovered how useful they were in the shop for making clean, precise, repeatable cuts. But the tool's useful portability has never gone away, and if you find yourself taking the saw to the job site, you'll want an easily transportable saw stand. A small folding stand is also advantageous in a small shop where space is at a premium.

This stand is designed for medium- and smaller-size miter saws, such as light-duty 7¼- and 10-inch models. It's also useful as a general-purpose utility table and can act as a sort of "side car" for your workbench. To keep its weight to a minimum, it forgoes extras, such as stock supports and leg levelers. Those can be added, but they will increase the weight and cost. For a small stand like this, it's best to use standalone stock supports. All of the lumber and hardware can be purchased at any home center and most hardware stores. Making the project is straightforward, but carefully following the assembly sequence is important to ensure the stand's sturdiness.

Material choices will make a difference in the weight and rigidity of the stand. Use a cabinet-grade plywood or MDF for the top.

(MDF is heavy, but it will provide a smooth, sturdy platform.) The leg and foot parts should be made of solid wood—the stiffer the better. Oak and maple are the best choices, but poplar and birch will also work well. The total cost of the project should be less than $60.

If you're tall, you might want to make the legs even longer to provide a more comfortable working height for the finished stand.

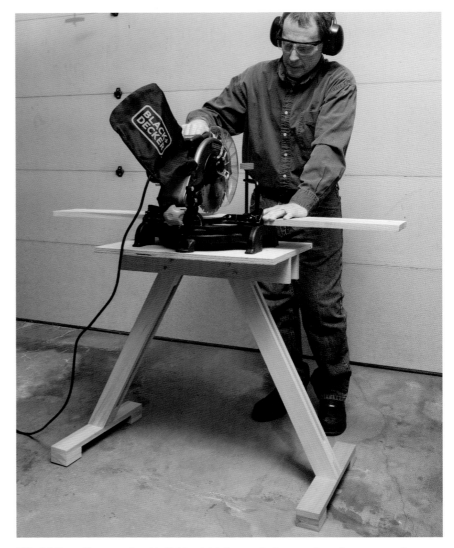

This folding miter saw stand is lightweight, is easy to transport, and can support any small- to medium-size saw. It can also double as a shop utility table. Fasten the miter saw to the stand with at least two bolts and wing nuts to keep it secured while working.

FOLDING MITER SAW STAND

TOOLS & MATERIALS

Eye & ear protection

Work gloves

1 × 3 × 96" solid wood (oak, poplar, pine, etc.) (4)

¾ × 24 × 24" birch plywood

Tablesaw or circular saw

Jigsaw

Cordless drill with ⅛" bit

Yellow wood glue

Pneumatic brad nailer (recommended)

1" pneumatic brads

C-clamps

Orbital sander

100-grit sandpaper

Miter saw

Combination square with protractor

Finish nails (1", 2")

No. 8 × 3" screws

⁵⁄₁₆ × 4½" bolts (2)

⁵⁄₁₆" flat washers (4)

⁵⁄₁₆" lock nuts (2)

Level

Permanent marker

¼ × 20 × 4" bolts (2)

¼ × 20 wing nuts (2)

8 × 2" screws

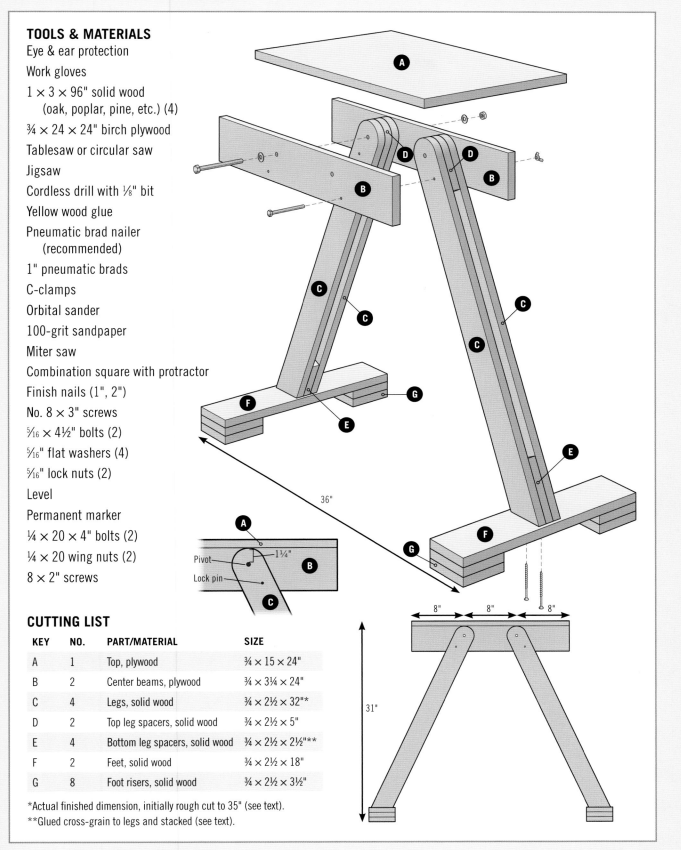

CUTTING LIST

KEY	NO.	PART/MATERIAL	SIZE
A	1	Top, plywood	¾ × 15 × 24"
B	2	Center beams, plywood	¾ × 3¼ × 24"
C	4	Legs, solid wood	¾ × 2½ × 32"*
D	2	Top leg spacers, solid wood	¾ × 2½ × 5"
E	4	Bottom leg spacers, solid wood	¾ × 2½ × 2½"**
F	2	Feet, solid wood	¾ × 2½ × 18"
G	8	Foot risers, solid wood	¾ × 2½ × 3½"

*Actual finished dimension, initially rough cut to 35" (see text).

**Glued cross-grain to legs and stacked (see text).

How to Make a Folding Miter Saw Stand

Cut the wood for the top, center beams, leg spacers, foot risers, and feet to size with a tablesaw or circular saw. Cut the legs to 35"; the finished length will be 32", but cut them long to allow for waste because of the cuts you'll make later. Mark the center pivot hole to round off the top of the legs, centered on the width of the boards and 1¼" down from the top. Use a pencil and compass to strike an arc from the marked centerpoint to the sides and top edge.

Clamp each leg to a workbench, and use a jigsaw with a narrow, fine-tooth blade to cut just outside the lines to allow a little extra stock for sanding later.

Use a ⅛" bit to bore a starter hole in the center of each leg. Be careful to drill the hole as close to perpendicular as possible. (After you've glued the legs and spacers together, you'll bore a larger hole through the assembled pieces for the bolt that allows the legs to pivot and fold.)

Glue the leg spacers between the legs, being careful to align the edges. (Don't worry about the square edge of the spacer protruding above the rounded top edges; you'll take care of this once the pieces are joined.) Note that the bottom legs spacers are glued cross-grain to the legs and there are two stacked together. Drive a few 1" brads (away from any future cuts) to prevent the parts from slipping, and then use C-clamps to hold them together until the glue cures.

④

Use the top rounded edges of the legs as a guide and, with a jigsaw, cut the protruding "ears" off the leg spacer so they are flush with the top of the legs (there's no need for them to be perfectly flush).

⑤

(continued)

Sand the rounded edges smooth with an orbital sander using 100-grit paper. Refine the arc so it is smooth and flush with the layout lines.

Now you need to cut the 25-degree miter on the bottom of the legs. Measure 32" from the top of the leg and use a combination square as a guide to mark squarely across the leg. (Remember, you can make the legs longer or shorter depending on the height you'd like the stand to be.) The longest side of the leg should be 32" long.

Now you can bore the full-size ⁵⁄₁₆" pivot holes for the bolts. Bore from each side so the holes meet in the middle.

Join the feet and foot risers together with 1" and 2" finish nails or pneumatic brads and glue. Clamp the pieces together while the glue dries. You can increase or reduce the number of risers to alter the height of the stand.

10

Now join the leg and feet assemblies together with glue and No. 8 × 3" screws driven through the bottom of the feet into the leg spacers.

11

Mark the pivot points on the beams 8" down from each end and centered on the board. Bore pilot holes in the beams, and then bore slightly oversized ¼" holes for the bolts. Check the fit to make sure the bolts pass easily through the beams and legs. Then insert the bolts with washers and fasten the lock nuts tight enough so the legs have sufficient resistance so they don't move on their own.

12

Now you need to set up the leg-locking mechanism. Place the leg-and-beam assembly so the feet rest flat on the ground; make sure both legs are at the same 25° angle to the center beams and that the beams are level. Use a marker to draw a line where the legs and beams meet. This will serve as an alignment guide when setting up the stand. Now, clamp the stand in position and bore holes for the ¼" locking bolts about halfway through the legs from each side, so they meet in the middle. When using the bench, these holes will be used for additional ¼" bolts and wing nuts that will prevent the legs from splaying.

13

On the bottom of the plywood top, outline the position of the leg-and-beam assembly with pencil. Turn the top right side up and rest it on the leg-and-beam assembly, aligning it with the marks. Mark the location for three or four screws for each half of the beam on the top of the stand. Use glue and countersunk 8 × 2" screws to attach the top to the beams. Smooth all sharp edges of the miter saw stand with sandpaper.

Bench-Top Router Table

The router is one of the most versatile tools you can own, but it's often misunderstood and underutilized. The router is great for handheld applications, but you can greatly expand its versatility by mounting it upside down in a router table. Although a router table can be as simple as a router mounted upside down on a board, you'd be missing out on features that add convenience, versatility, and safety. Compact bench-top tables make the most sense because their worksurface is appropriate for the kind of jobs routers are meant to do and they can be stored out of the way when not in use. If you already have a workbench, a floor-standing router table is a waste of space.

This router table is designed to accommodate most medium to large-size routers. Before making this table, check to see whether there are any restrictions on your router for this sort of mounting. It doesn't matter whether you use a fixed base or a plunge router—either type will work well.

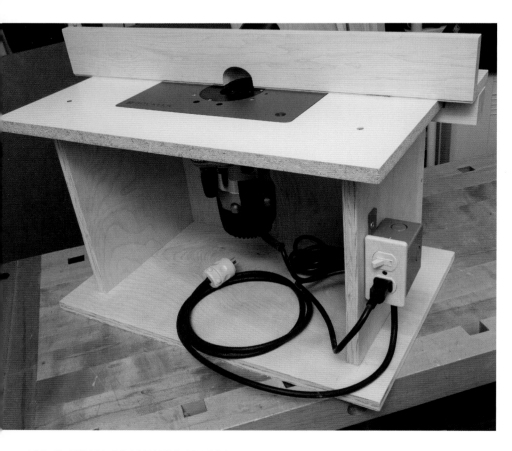

This router table is suitable for almost any size router and incorporates a no-sag mounting plate and a versatile fence with integral dust collection.

BENCH-TOP ROUTER TABLE

TOOLS & MATERIALS

Eye & ear protection

Work gloves

Hole saw (if making insert)

Tablesaw

24 × 48" birch plywood
(or equivalent) (1)

Orbital sander

120- or 150-grit sandpaper

Yellow wood glue

Cordless drill

C-clamps

Tape measure and pencil

No. 8 × 2½" screws

No. 6 × ¾" washer-head
screws

Melamine-coated MDF
or particleboard

Router table insert

Router and ¼" shank pattern
router bit, ½" dia. × ¼"

Router plate template

1" × 4 × 6' hardwood
for fence parts (1)

⁵⁄₁₆ × 3½" carriage bolts (2)

⁵⁄₁₆" T-knobs (2)

⁵⁄₁₆" flat washers (2)

Rubber cushion for fence
clamps (rubber stair tread,
rubber gasket material) (2)

Contact cement

Dust collection port

Duplex electrical box (optional)

Electrical switch/outlet
combination

14/3 electrical cord
(10' maximum)

Three-prong grounded plug

Outlet cover

Cable clamp

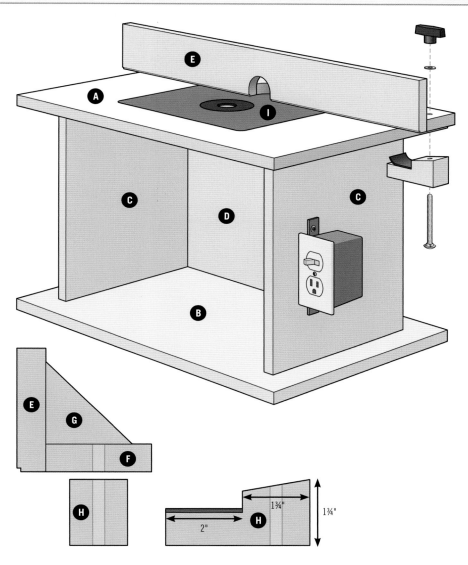

CUTTING LIST

KEY	NO.	PART/MATERIAL	SIZE
A	1	Top, melamine-coated MDF	¾ × 16 × 24"
B	1	Base, plywood	¾ × 16 × 24"
C	2	Sides, plywood	¾ × 12 × 13½"
D	1	Back, plywood	¾ × 13½ × 18½"
E	1	Fence front, hardwood	¾ × 3⅜ × 27½"
F	1	Fence base, hardwood	¾ × 2¾ × 27½"
G	2	Fence gussets, hardwood	¾ × 2¼ × 2¼"*
H	2	Fence clamps, hardwood	1½ × 1¾ × 3¾"
I	1	Table insert	⅜ × 9¼ × 11¾"**

*Triangular piece.

**Commercially made table inserts are available online. Size given is typical.

HOW TO MAKE YOUR OWN INSERT PLATE

If you purchase an insert (highly recommended and shown in the photos), follow the supplied installation instructions. The instructions will vary depending on the manufacturer. But if you make your own insert plate out of ⅜" polycarbonate, you'll need to make this before cutting the hole in the tabletop.

Along with a tablesaw, you'll need a hole saw to cut the center opening in the plate where the router bit will fit, and a ⅜" rabbeting bit with a ball-bearing pilot to cut the rabbet in the top for the insert. It's also a good idea to round off the insert's outside corners so they won't snag on workpieces.

When cutting plastic, use slower cutting speeds to avoid melting the material. Polycarbonate is even more difficult because it doesn't cut easily—it's very hard and brittle and tends to chip. Be sure to use a jigsaw blade that is specifically made to cut plastic.

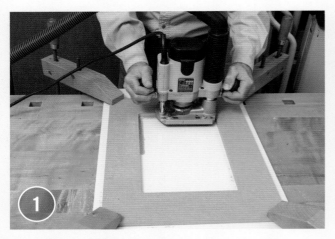

To rout the rabbet in the top that holds the router mounting insert plate, you'll need an exact-size template and a top-bearing, flush-trim pattern bit. This MDF template is made specifically to produce a perfect fit for the manufactured phenolic plate.

Check the depth of the cut to match the thickness of the mounting plate with a caliper or combination square, or make a gauge with a stick and block. It's important that the depth exactly matches the thickness of the plate so it will be perfectly level with the top.

Bore holes in each corner to round the edges and to create starting points for cutting out the center with a jigsaw. Elevate the top and use a backup block under the holes to prevent chip-out damage. Note that the holes are bored on the outside edge of the cut.

Cut out the center with a jigsaw by sawing along the melamine outside of the rabbet. You could also use a straightedge for a cleaner cut. When you're finished cutting, clean up the edges with sandpaper.

Attach the router to the mounting plate and be sure it's oriented correctly. Pre-drilled, commercially made plates are available for almost every router. Phenolic or aluminum are the best plate materials because, while they are thin, they don't sag under the weight of a router.

Cut the bit/dust-collection opening in the fence front with a jigsaw and then mark the corresponding location on the fence base. The size of the opening should be large enough so it doesn't interfere with router operation.

Use a jigsaw and a narrow blade to cut the dust-opening in the fence base. Go slow; it's a tight curve, so you might need to make relief cuts. Clean up the cut with sandpaper or a file.

To prevent sawdust from building up along the bottom edge of the fence while routing, cut a small rabbet along its length on the table saw. The depth should be about $1/16$" and the height about $1/8$".

Glue the fence halves together and clamp them with wooden handscrews. To keep them perfectly aligned, you can use dowels, biscuits, or brads. Don't over-tighten the clamps and leave them on for at least three hours to allow the glue to set.

(continued)

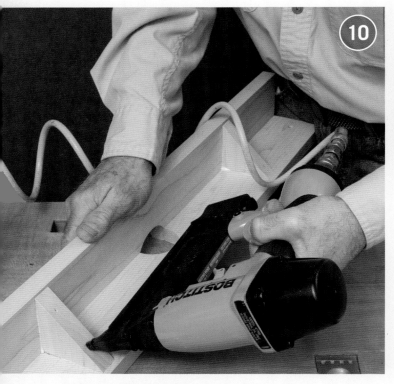

Fasten the fence gussets with glue and pneumatic brads. The gussets keep the front fence square and prevent flexing under load.

Lay out the fence clamps on a single (or glued-together) block of wood. Before cutting the shapes, bore the 5/16" holes for the carriage bolts. You can cut clamps with a jigsaw, but a bandsaw provides more control and a smoother cut.

Glue the rubber friction pads to the fence clamps with contact cement. These pads are made from rubber gasket that's available at most hardware stores. The pads provide the grip that prevents the fence from slipping when work is pushed against it.

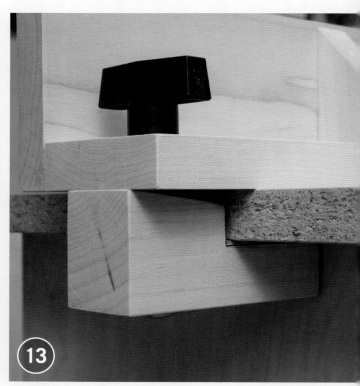

The angle cut into the fence clamp allows it to pivot and tighten, so the leg with the rubber pad can provide a secure grip on the top.

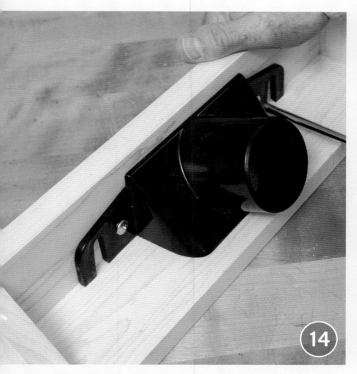

14

15

Screw the dust-collection port to the back of the fence with washer-head screws. Ports such as this one are available from many online retailers. The port size is compatible with many shop vacuums, and adaptors are also available.

The stand is simply glued and screwed together. After assembling the sides and back, attach the base with screws driven through the bottom. If you want a cleaner look, you could join the parts with biscuits or dowels.

16

17

After boring clearance holes and countersinks, align the top with the stand and hold it in place with the points of a few screws. Then bore pilot holes and drive screws. You could also use metal L-brackets to attach the top from the bottom. Don't use glue, however, because you may need to replace the top at some point.

Although it's optional, a switched outlet makes it easier, faster, and safer to control the router. The wire must be at least the same gauge as the router's. There are commercially available prewired switches if you don't feel confident doing the wiring yourself.

Wall Tool Cabinet

Storing commonly used tools on a shop wall is convenient, efficient, and intuitive. Slot wall and pegboard are the most popular systems, but pegboard is far and away the most economical, because the panels and hangers are a fraction of the cost of equivalent slot wall systems. But small shops often don't have an abundance of wall space, and if that's the situation in your shop, there is a workaround. This wall-mounted tool cabinet effectively triples the wall space, and it provides protection for the tools stored inside. The cabinet's depth is less than 7 inches, so it's unlikely to interfere with your work. You'll want to mount the cabinet in a spot where it spans two wall studs in order to anchor it securely.

A tablesaw is a must-have tool for this project. Although there's nothing complex about building the cabinet, there are several rip cuts that are best done on a tablesaw. If you want to save time, a plate joiner will speed the door construction and a pneumatic brad nailer is much faster than driving nails with a hammer. Poplar is a good material for this cabinet because it's easy to work, knot free, not prone to warping, and inexpensive. Other suitable milled board stock that are commonly available at home centers include maple, oak, birch, and clear pine. The total cost of the project should be well under $70.

With storage behind and inside the doors, this pegboard wall cabinet is ideal for small shops because it can store three times as much as a single pegboard but takes up the same amount of space.

WALL TOOL CABINET

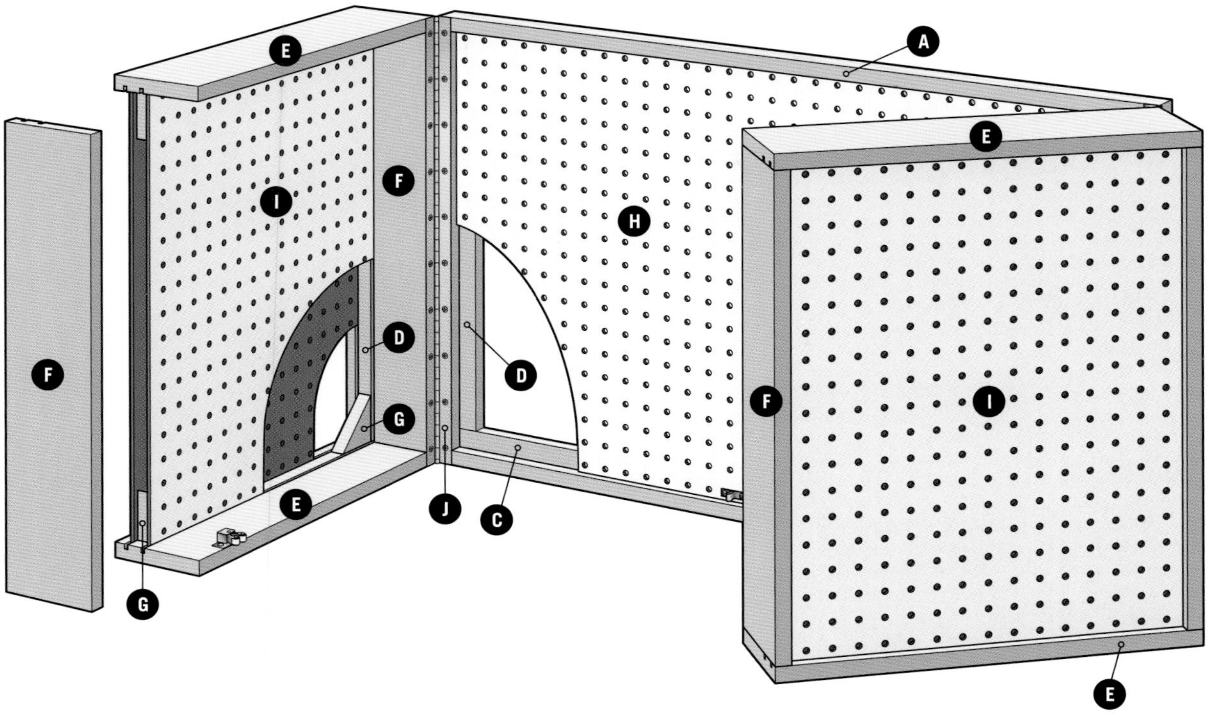

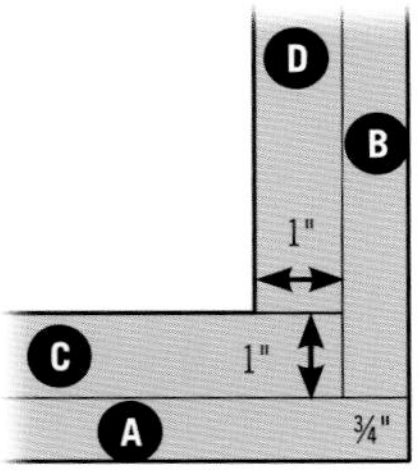

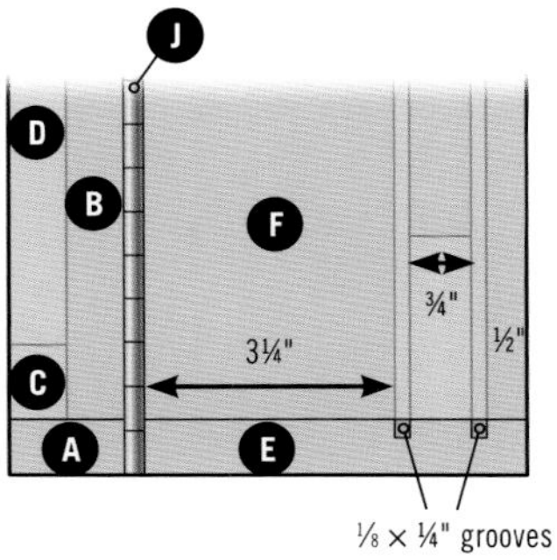

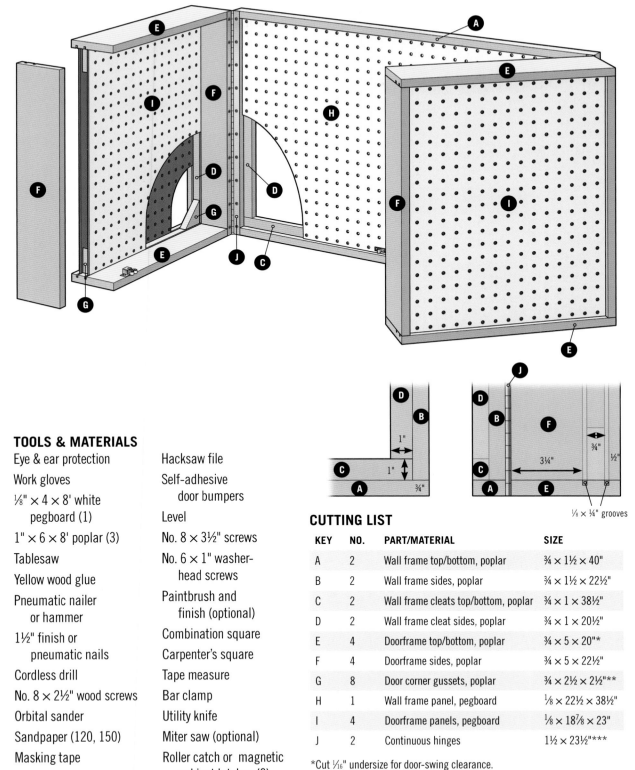

TOOLS & MATERIALS

- Eye & ear protection
- Work gloves
- ⅛" × 4 × 8' white pegboard (1)
- 1" × 6 × 8' poplar (3)
- Tablesaw
- Yellow wood glue
- Pneumatic nailer or hammer
- 1½" finish or pneumatic nails
- Cordless drill
- No. 8 × 2½" wood screws
- Orbital sander
- Sandpaper (120, 150)
- Masking tape
- 1½ × 48" piano hinge (continuous hinge)
- Hacksaw file
- Self-adhesive door bumpers
- Level
- No. 8 × 3½" screws
- No. 6 × 1" washer-head screws
- Paintbrush and finish (optional)
- Combination square
- Carpenter's square
- Tape measure
- Bar clamp
- Utility knife
- Miter saw (optional)
- Roller catch or magnetic cabinet latches (2)

CUTTING LIST

KEY	NO.	PART/MATERIAL	SIZE
A	2	Wall frame top/bottom, poplar	¾ × 1½ × 40"
B	2	Wall frame sides, poplar	¾ × 1½ × 22½"
C	2	Wall frame cleats top/bottom, poplar	¾ × 1 × 38½"
D	2	Wall frame cleat sides, poplar	¾ × 1 × 20½"
E	4	Doorframe top/bottom, poplar	¾ × 5 × 20"*
F	4	Doorframe sides, poplar	¾ × 5 × 22½"
G	8	Door corner gussets, poplar	¾ × 2½ × 2½"**
H	1	Wall frame panel, pegboard	⅛ × 22½ × 38½"
I	4	Doorframe panels, pegboard	⅛ × 18⅞ × 23"
J	2	Continuous hinges	1½ × 23½"***

*Cut 1/16" undersize for door-swing clearance.

**Triangular parts.

***Two sections cut from one 48"-long hinge.

How to Make a Wall Tool Cabinet

Cut all parts from the pegboard and poplar with a tablesaw. Attach the cleats to the top, bottom, and sides using glue and 1½" finish nails. Note that the top and bottom frame cleats terminate ¾" from the ends, while the side cleats end 1" from the ends of their mating pieces.

Position the frame parts together and drive a few nails to hold them together. Then bore countersunk pilot holes and secure each corner with No. 8 × 2½" screws. Use the back pegboard to keep the frame square while you're assembling it. Sand the parts quickly with 150-grit sandpaper and ease all the sharp edges.

To build the doors, start by marking each piece and how it orients to the mating parts, using masking tape labels.

Now, bore clearance holes and countersinks in the top and bottom parts (two screws in each joint). The screw holes must not be in line with the pegboard panels. Line up the tops and bottoms with their mating sides and bore pilot holes.

5

Next, cut the grooves in the frame parts for the pegboard panels. Most tablesaw blades have a ⅛" kerf, so one or two passes over the blade should do the trick. Refer to the drawing for the distance between cuts.

6

Glue and nail the doorframes for alignment. At this point you should only assemble the bottom and two sides.

7

Bore pilot holes into the sides. In solid wood, the bit diameter should be slightly less than the diameter of the screw.

8

Set the drill's clutch to prevent overdriving or stripping the screws, and then secure the sides to the bottom with wood screws. Don't install the top just yet. *(continued)*

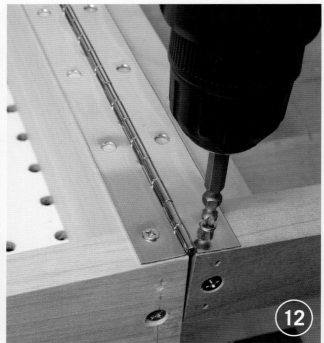

Test-fit the door panels and gussets. It's easier to do a preliminary sanding before assembly, so use an orbital sander with 120-grit sandpaper to quickly remove any roughness. Slide in the front panel, and then glue and nail the corner gussets into the assembled bottom and side pieces.

Glue and nail the gussets on the open end of the sides, where the top will fit. Make sure that the gussets are perfectly flush with the ends of the side and do not overlap the grooves.

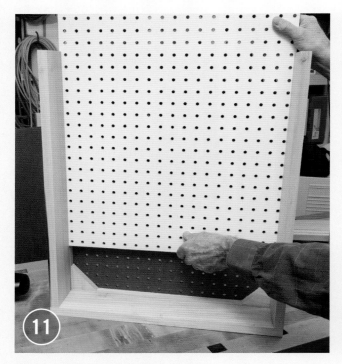

Apply a small amount of glue to the slots, and then slide in the inside pegboard panel. Position the top doorframe in place and check the fit. Finish the door by gluing and screwing on the top to the sides and gussets. Check to make sure the door is square and rests flat. You can torque the door at the corners, if necessary, or use a bar clamp to apply pressure across the joints to square it up.

Cut the 48" piano hinge in half with a hacksaw and use a file to ease sharp edges. Install the piano hinge to the door and wall frame with just a few screws at first. Note that the hinge's barrel is located just outside the door and frame edges. The hinge barrel should extend past the edge of the frame pieces. Check that the doors will close squarely against the frame. Once you're satisfied with the fit, remove the hinge from the wall frame.

Place self-adhesive bumpers on the inside edges of the doors. The bumpers are about the same thickness as the piano hinge, so they balance the door gap.

Mount the wall frame to the wall by first using a level to strike a line corresponding to the top or bottom of the frame. Locate two wall studs that fall within the frame and mark them. Place the frame against the wall and drive at least two No. 8 × 3½" screws through the frame cleats into the studs.

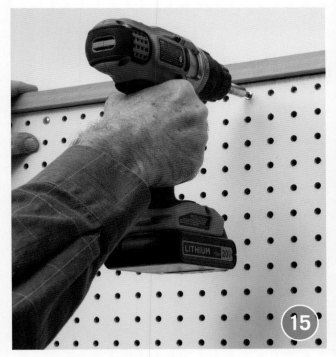

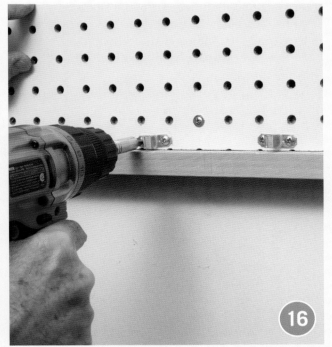

Use washer-head screws to secure the pegboard to the frame cleats. Use about five screws on the top and bottom and about three down the sides. Now you can remount the door to the frame. Install enough screws in the hinges to support the doors and adjust the alignment to the frame if needed. Then finish driving all the screws.

The final step is to install the roller latches and catches. You could also use magnetic push latches or even hooks on the outside. You can leave the cabinet unfinished or apply a finish, such as a clear water-based polyurethane varnish.

Tablesaw Cross-Cut Sled

The built-in accuracy of any saw can take you only so far when you're trying to cut precisely. To achieve an accurate rip cut on a tablesaw, it must have a fence that locks securely and is perfectly parallel with the blade. Most decent tablesaws meet that requirement, but the standard miter gauge for making cross-cuts typically lacks precision and capacity, and it can't begin to handle larger workpieces.

A tablesaw cross-cut sled (sliding cutoff table) provides the capacity and accuracy you'll need for many woodworking projects, and it's a relatively simple device to build. Much of its assembly happens right on the saw table, because it needs to be a match with the parts on your saw. The drawing and cut list are for reference only because of the differences in saw table sizes and the varying distance between miter gauge slots. For the sled to work properly, the blade must be perfectly parallel with the slots. If necessary, the arbor on most saws can be adjusted to bring it into alignment with the slots. Refer to your saw's instruction manual. If your tool is a contractor-style or stationary saw, the size of the sled will be about right. Note that this sled is not designed to cut compound miters, but you can cut simple miters by adding fences to the base.

The quality of the materials for this project should be cabinet-grade plywood, not construction grade. The best is baltic birch plywood or a similar multi-ply void-free material. The density, flatness, and dimensional stability of baltic birch ensure the sled will remain accurate and be durable. For the fence cores, use ¾-inch particleboard or MDF, and a dense hardwood, such as maple or cherry, for the runners. The key to building a good sled is to eliminate any play or wobble, and that comes down to how well the runners fit in the miter slots. Select wood with straight grain and no knots or flaws.

A tablesaw cutoff sled lets you make perfect cuts in small to large stock without the risk of kickback that a miter gauge might present. This design can be scaled to fit any saw.

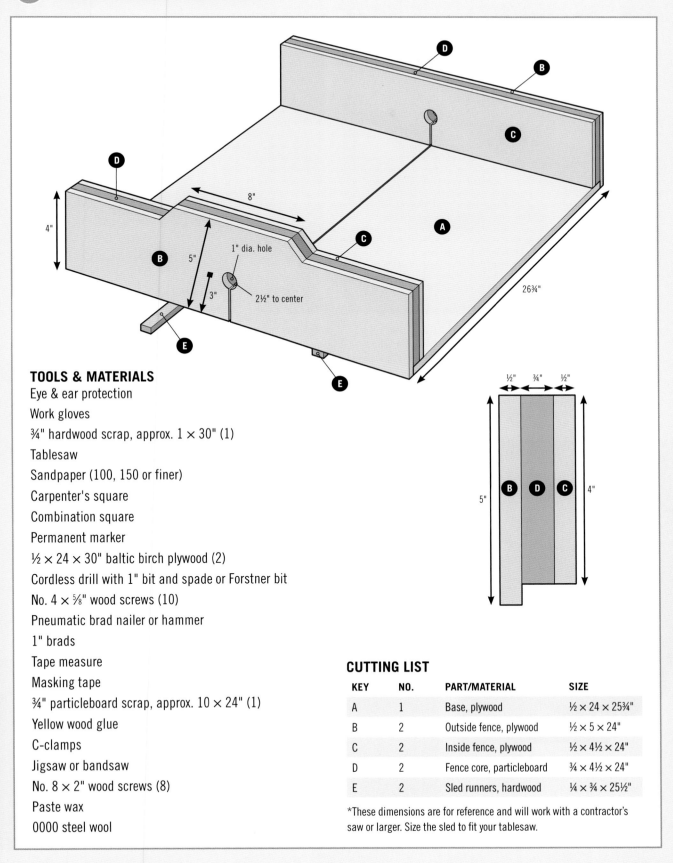

TOOLS & MATERIALS

Eye & ear protection

Work gloves

¾" hardwood scrap, approx. 1 × 30" (1)

Tablesaw

Sandpaper (100, 150 or finer)

Carpenter's square

Combination square

Permanent marker

½ × 24 × 30" baltic birch plywood (2)

Cordless drill with 1" bit and spade or Forstner bit

No. 4 × ⅝" wood screws (10)

Pneumatic brad nailer or hammer

1" brads

Tape measure

Masking tape

¾" particleboard scrap, approx. 10 × 24" (1)

Yellow wood glue

C-clamps

Jigsaw or bandsaw

No. 8 × 2" wood screws (8)

Paste wax

0000 steel wool

CUTTING LIST

KEY	NO.	PART/MATERIAL	SIZE
A	1	Base, plywood	½ × 24 × 25¾"
B	2	Outside fence, plywood	½ × 5 × 24"
C	2	Inside fence, plywood	½ × 4½ × 24"
D	2	Fence core, particleboard	¾ × 4½ × 24"
E	2	Sled runners, hardwood	¼ × ¾ × 25½"

*These dimensions are for reference and will work with a contractor's saw or larger. Size the sled to fit your tablesaw.

How to Make a Tablesaw Cross-Cut Sled

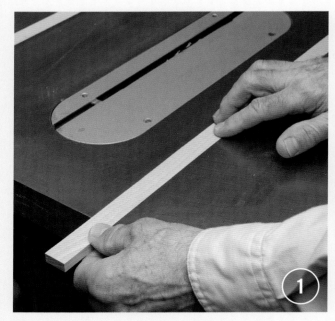

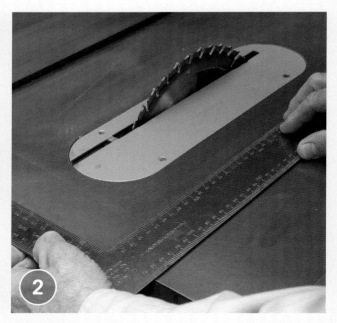

With a tablesaw, cut the hardwood pieces for the runners so they're a tight fit in the slots on the table of your saw. Then refine the fit by sanding until they fit snugly but can still slide freely in the slots. It's actually an advantage if the thickness of the runners is slightly less than the depth of the miter slots. This will allow them to ride over any dust that accumulates in the slots but still be able push dust out as it builds up.

With a carpenter's square, check to see if the miter slots are perpendicular to the edge of the table. If they are, then construction will be a little easier. If not, though, use indelible marker to draw a line across the table of the saw, as close as possible to the end of the table and exactly perpendicular to the miter slots.

Lower the tablesaw blade below the surface of the table, and then place the runners in the miter slots. Position the saw sled base on the table; if the edge of the saw was perpendicular to the miter slots, then position the base so the front edge is perfectly aligned with the edge of the table. But if the table was out of square with the miter slots, then position the base flush along the line you marked across the top of the saw table. Mark a line on the edge of the base, corresponding to the exact center of the runners.

Check to make sure the blade is exactly in line with the miter slots. If not, adjust it until it is in perfect alignment. Now, cut the sled base from plywood to the same length as the saw table. Now cut the base of the saw table sled to exactly match the width of your saw table.

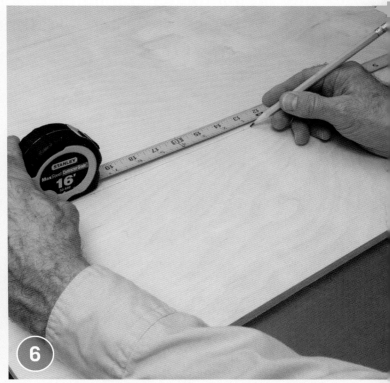

Position the sled base precisely over the runners, then use a combination square as a guide to draw lines on the top of the base to mark the centerlines of the runners.

On the runner centerlines, mark five positions for evenly spaced countersink holes for the No. 4 × ⅝" screws that will secure the runners to the bottom of the sled.

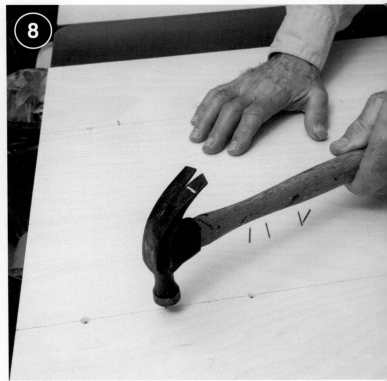

Bore the countersunk pilot holes along the marked points. Make the counterbores a little deep so that the screws will have more bite in the runners.

Temporarily tack the sled base down into the runners with 1" brads to hold the pieces in place. Check to make sure the sled slides back and forth freely along the saw table. *(continued)*

Now drill pilot holes down through the countersinks. A tape guide around your drill bit will help you avoid drilling all the way down through the runners.

Drive wood screws at the pilot holes to secure the sled base to the runners. Check again to make sure the sled slides smoothly back and forth across the saw table.

Measure, mark, and cut the pieces of plywood and particleboard for the front and back fences of the sled, as shown in the plan drawings. Next, glue and clamp the parts together with C-clamps. You can use a few brads to keep the parts from sliding around before clamping.

After the glue dries, remove the clamps and cut the 1" stress-relief holes on the front and back fences, centered between the runners and positioned 2⅝" up from the bottoms, using a spade bit or Forstner bit. To avoid splintering, drill partway through one face, then turn the piece over and drill through the opposite side to complete the hole.

Use a jigsaw or bandsaw to trim the ends and the top edge of the back fence, if needed. The front fence gets a special treatment with a center "hump" cut in it—a safety feature to position your hands away from the blade. Lay out the hump and cut it with a jigsaw or a bandsaw.

To attach the fences to the base with glue and screws, first position the pieces in a dry fit, making sure they're square with the saw centerline and to the base. Now, bore the clearance holes and countersinks for four No. 8 × 2" wood screws in each end of the base.

Take special care with the front fence because it's the one that guides the stock. Apply glue, drive four No. 8 × 2" screws, and check for square again. Position the sled on the saw and run it back and forth to make sure it's sliding smoothly. Make any adjustments to the runners with fine sandpaper and then use paste wax and 0000 steel wool to polish them.

To cut the kerf down the length of the base, position the back fence in front of the blade, raised just enough to cut through the base. Turn on the saw and move the sled through the blade, cutting the base from end to end. Now raise the blade to full height and cut again. Remove the sled and smooth all the sharp edges with 100-grit sandpaper. Finally, cut a few boards and check them for square.

Resources

www.rockler.com

Bench-top router table project:
Phenolic table insert (item is specific to different router models):
   www.rockler.com/rockler-phenolic-router-plates
Router plate template (item #20956):
   www.rockler.com/rockler-router-plate-template
Pattern router bit - ½" dia × ¼" H × ¼" shank:
   www.rockler.com/1-2-pattern-router-bit
Router table dust port (item #21528):
   www.rockler.com/router-table-dust-port

Downdraft sanding table project:
Universal dust port (item #92031):
   www.rockler.com/universal-dust-port

Dust-collection hose adaptors shown in various photos:
Dust Right Universal hose kit (item #48212):
   www.rockler.com/dust-right-universal-small-port-hose-kit

Free access to National Electrical Codes:
www.nfpa.org/freeaccess

Online information on dust collection:
www.rockler.com/skill-builders/setting-up-your-shop/dust-collection-
   system-design-and-equipment
www.oneida-air.com/static.asp?htmltemplate=static/ductwork_
   tutorial01.html
www.highlandwoodworking.com/smallshopdustcollectionsimplified.
   aspx

Safety products and information:
www.3m.com/3M/en_US/company-us/all-3m-products/~/All-3M-
   Products/Consumer/Home-Improvement/3M-Safety/?N=5002385+
   8709316+8740610+8743715+3294857497&rt=r3

Acknowledgments

People who allowed me to photograph their shops:
Brian Baldwin
Brian Deick
Marke Lane
Laura Lane
Bob Lundstrom
Les Minor
Lynn Norton
Jim Strand

Additional photo credits (for shop photos):
Marke Lane
Lynn Norton

Photography models and assistants:
Andrea Baldwin
Mark Ferris
Laura Lane
Janice Watkins

Photo Credits

Flow Wall: 20

iStock: 43

Shutterstock: 10, 12, 14 (top), 41, 57 (bottom right), 61 (top), 68 (bottom), 70 (bottom right), 71 (top), 82 (bottom left), 88–89

Metric Conversion Charts

CONVERTING MEASUREMENTS

TO CONVERT:	TO:	MULTIPLY BY:
Inches	Millimeters	25.4
Inches	Centimeters	2.54
Feet	Meters	0.305
Yards	Meters	0.914
Square inches	Square centimeters	6.45
Square feet	Square meters	0.093
Square yards	Square meters	0.836
Cubic inches	Cubic centimeters	16.4
Cubic feet	Cubic meters	0.0283
Cubic yards	Cubic meters	0.765
Pounds	Kilograms	0.454

TO CONVERT:	TO:	MULTIPLY BY:
Millimeters	Inches	0.039
Centimeters	Inches	0.394
Meters	Feet	3.28
Meters	Yards	1.09
Square centimeters	Square inches	0.155
Square meters	Square feet	10.8
Square meters	Square yards	1.2
Cubic centimeters	Cubic inches	0.061
Cubic meters	Cubic feet	35.3
Cubic meters	Cubic yards	1.31
Kilograms	Pounds	2.2

LUMBER DIMENSIONS

NOMINAL - U.S.	ACTUAL - U.S. (IN INCHES)	METRIC
1 × 2	¾ × 1½	19 × 38 mm
1 × 3	¾ × 2½	19 × 64 mm
1 × 4	¾ × 3½	19 × 89 mm
1 × 6	¾ × 5½	19 × 140 mm
1 × 8	¾ × 7¼	19 × 184 mm
1 × 10	¾ × 9¼	19 × 235 mm
1 × 12	¾ × 11¼	19 × 286 mm
2 × 2	1½ × 1½	38 × 38 mm
2 × 3	1½ × 2½	38 × 64 mm

NOMINAL - U.S.	ACTUAL - U.S. (IN INCHES)	METRIC
2 × 4	1½ × 3½	38 × 89 mm
2 × 6	1½ × 5½	38 × 140 mm
2 × 8	1½ × 7¼	38 × 184 mm
2 × 10	1½ × 9¼	38 × 235 mm
2 × 12	1½ × 11¼	38 × 286 mm
4 × 4	3½ × 3½	89 × 89 mm
4 × 6	3½ × 5½	89 × 140 mm
6 × 6	5½ × 5½	140 × 140 mm
8 × 8	7¼ × 7¼	184 × 184 mm

METRIC PLYWOOD

STANDARD SHEATHING GRADE	SANDED GRADE
7.5 mm (5⁄16")	6 mm (4⁄17")
9.5 mm (3⁄8")	8 mm (5⁄16")
12.5 mm (1⁄2")	11 mm (7⁄16")
15.5 mm (5⁄8")	14 mm (9⁄16")
18.5 mm (3⁄4")	17 mm (2⁄3")
20.5 mm (13⁄16")	19 mm (3⁄4")
22.5 mm (7⁄8")	21 mm (13⁄16")
25.5 mm (1")	24 mm (15⁄16")

COUNTERBORE, SHANK & PILOT HOLE DIAMETERS (INCHES)

SCREW SIZE	COUNTERBORE DIAMETER FOR SCREW HEAD	CLEARANCE HOLE FOR SCREW SHANK	PILOT HOLE DIAMETER	
			HARD WOOD	SOFT WOOD
#1	.146 (9⁄64)	5⁄64	3⁄64	1⁄32
#2	¼	3⁄32	3⁄64	1⁄32
#3	¼	7⁄64	1⁄16	3⁄64
#4	¼	1⁄8	1⁄16	3⁄64
#5	¼	1⁄8	5⁄64	1⁄16
#6	5⁄16	9⁄64	3⁄32	5⁄64
#7	5⁄16	5⁄32	3⁄32	5⁄64
#8	3⁄8	11⁄64	1⁄8	3⁄32
#9	3⁄8	11⁄64	1⁄8	3⁄32
#10	3⁄8	3⁄16	1⁄8	7⁄64
#11	½	3⁄16	5⁄32	9⁄64
#12	½	7⁄32	9⁄64	1⁄8

Index